Organize Your Per...

Finances

...In No Time

Debbie Stanley

que

800 East 96th Street
Indianapolis, Indiana 46240

Executive Editor
Candace Hall

Development Editor
Lorna Gentry

Managing Editor
Charlotte Clapp

Project Editor
Tonya Simpson

Production Editor
Megan Wade

Indexer
Chris Barrick

Proofreader
Jennifer Timpe

Technical Editor
Kate Rhoad

Publishing Coordinator
Cindy Teeters

Designer
Anne Jones

Page Layout
Stacey Richwine-DeRome
Julie Parks

Contents at a Glance

Introduction 1

Part I   **Capture the Numbers** **7**
    1   Tracking Your Money 9
    2   Getting the Figures to Match 29
    3   Avoiding Late Fees and Overdrafts 47

Part II   **Corral the Paper** **63**
    4   Fighting the Data Deluge 65
    5   Here to Stay: Storing Documents for Easy Retrieval 77
    6   Proving It's Yours, Or Should Be 97

Part III   **Advanced Projects** **109**
    7   Be an Organized Consumer 111
    8   Learn More from Your Organized Data 125

Conclusion 139
Appendix A   Further Resources 143
Appendix B   Sample Finance Forms 149
Index 155

Table of Contents

Introduction 1

I Capture the Numbers

1 Tracking Your Money **9**

Getting Your Mind Around the Task Ahead 10

Arming Yourself with the Right Organization System 11

Building a Fence to Snare Every Last Scrap of Your Financial
    Information 12
    Changing Habits 13
    Choosing the Gathering Place 16
    Tracking Cash, With or Without Receipts 16
    Recording Every Transaction, Even When You're Rushed 17

Creating an Income and Expense Tracking Document 20
    Laying the Foundation 20
    Setting Up the Income Section 22
    Setting Up the Expenses Section 23
    Seeing the Big Picture 25

Managing Joint Accounts: A Five-Point Peace Plan 26

Summary 28

2 Getting the Figures to Match **29**

Learning to Reconcile Your Accounts the Old-Fashioned Way 30
    The Basic Idea 31
    The Basic Steps 32
    Troubleshooting to Find Discrepancies 33

Letting Your Computer Do the Work 35
    Financial Software Options 35
    Choosing and Setting Up Your Software Product 37

Backing Up Financial Data on Your Computer 41
    Choosing a Backup Method 41
    Deciding Which Files to Back Up 42
    Storing Your Backup Disks 43
    Using a Disk-Free Option: Online Storage 44

Summary 46

3 Avoiding Late Fees and Overdrafts 47

When Time Flies, So Does Money: Finding a System for On-Time
Payments 48
What Makes This So Hard for You? 49
Are You a Sprinter or a Jogger? 49
What Has Worked in the Past? 50
What Do You Do Now to Finally Get It Done? 50
Doing Damage Control with "Safety Valve" Accounts 50

Finding the Best Way to Pay 52

Less Painful Bill-Paying 53
Option 1: An All-Paper System 54
Option 2: A Software-Based System 57
Option 3: A Web-Based System 58
Sticking with Your System 59

Summary 61

II Corral the Paper

4 Fighting the Data Deluge 65

Incoming! Taking Control of Paper at the Point of Entry 66
Step 1: Get Rid of the Junk 67
Step 2: Put Financial Mail Where It Belongs 73
Step 3: Pass on Others' Mail 73
Step 4: Put Magazines, Catalogs, and Packages Where They Belong .. 73
Step 5: Deal with the Leftovers 74

What about Incoming Paper from Other Sources? 75
Paperwork from Others in Your Household 75
Dealing with Odds and Ends 75

Summary 76

5 Here to Stay: Storing Documents for Easy Retrieval .. 77

File or Pile? Choosing Paper Storage Options 78
Piling Might Be Right 79
The Best of Both Worlds 80

Step 1: Divide Your Documents into Groups 82
Sorting Out Documents for Frequent Files 84
Setting Aside Other Groups 84

A Quick Lesson in Categorizing 86
    Categorizing Is Better Than Alphabetizing 86
    Think in Terms of "Which Is Bigger?" 87
    Use Your Own Words 87
    Keeping Categories Under Control 88

Step 2: Subdivide Your Frequent Files Group
    into Categories 88

Step 3: Label Your Folders and Start Filing! 90
    A Neat Trick with Hanging Folders 90
    Filing Your Documents 91

Step 4: Create Archive Files 92
    Separating Documents for Archiving 93
    Storing the Archived Documents 95

Summary 95

6 Proving It's Yours, Or Should Be **97**

Building Your Room-by-Room Files 98
    Gathering File Contents 100
    Listing Your Spaces 100
    Making Your Files 101
    Categorizing Room-by-Room Files 101
    Filing Your Documents 102
    Maintaining the System 103

Creating a Property Inventory 104
    Taping It 104
    Writing It 106
    Maintaining It 107

Summary 107

III Advanced Projects

7 Be an Organized Consumer **111**

No More Roaming the Aisles 112

Reducing Bulky Catalog Clutter 114

Becoming a Master Listmaker for More Organized Shopping 117
    Listing Things You Need and Things You Already Have 117
    Who Wants What: Maintaining Gift Lists 119

Never Again Wonder, "Did I Get That?" 122

Summary 123

8 Learn More from Your Organized Data **125**

Calculating Your Personal Profits and Losses 126

Getting In-Depth with Your Debt 128

Taking a Close Look at Your Spending Patterns 130

Do You Live Beyond Your Means? 131

Using Your Data to Organize a Budget 133
  Beginning at the Beginning 133
  Designing Your Budget 134
  Trimming Expenses Gets Easier 136

Summary 138

Conclusion **139**

The "Just Do It" Factor 139

Use Your System 140
  Have a Home 140
  Be Consistent 141
  Be Organized Enough 141

Farewell 142

Appendix A Further Resources **143**

Products and Services Recommended in This Book 144
  Books 144
  Data Management Products and Services 144
  Junk Mail Management Services 144
  Money Management Products 144
  Organizing Products 145

Financial Information and Counseling 145

Professional Organizing Information and Referrals 148

Appendix B Sample Finance Forms **149**

Index **155**

About the Author

Debbie Stanley transitioned from a successful career in journalism and reference publishing to the highly rewarding role of professional organizer and coach for chronically disorganized clients. The owner of Red Letter Day Professional Organizers (www.RLDPO.com), Stanley's work is informed by a bachelor's degree in journalism and a master's in industrial/organizational psychology. Stanley contributes to the growth of her industry as a trainer to fellow organizers and as a speaker to groups, including Children and Adults with Attention Deficit/Hyperactivity Disorder (CHADD). She is the chair of the National Association of Professional Organizers' Publications Committee and president of NAPO's Southeast Michigan chapter. Stanley is also a past board member of and active participant in the National Study Group on Chronic Disorganization (NSGCD) and has earned the NSGCD's Chronic Disorganization Specialist certificate.

Dedication

To Bethany and Michael

Acknowledgments

As the National Association of Professional Organizers says, "Together we are better." I couldn't do what I do without these folks:

My clients: You are amazing! Every one of you has taught me something, and in doing so you've helped each other as well. It is a privilege to work with you.

My peers: I'm fortunate to be part of an industry that values cooperation and sharing for the good of us all. Many thanks to everyone who has served on a committee with me, worked on a project, or developed new ideas over a meal at the NAPO Conference.

My Que team: Your diligence and depth of experience have been mightily comforting to me. Thank you for making this a pleasant and productive publishing experience.

My friends and family: You're the only ones who can make me realize when it really is time to take a break. Thanks for keeping me balanced by celebrating what a cool job I have and still dragging me away from it once in a while.

We Want to Hear from You!

As the reader of this book, *you* are our most important critic and commentator. We value your opinion and want to know what we're doing right, what we could do better, what areas you'd like to see us publish in, and any other words of wisdom you're willing to pass our way.

As an executive editor for Que, I welcome your comments. You can email or write me directly to let me know what you did or didn't like about this book—as well as what we can do to make our books better.

Please note that I cannot help you with technical problems related to the topic of this book. We do have a User Services group, however, where I will forward specific technical questions related to the book.

When you write, please be sure to include this book's title and author as well as your name, email address, and phone number. I will carefully review your comments and share them with the author and editors who worked on the book.

Email: feedback@quepublishing.com

Mail: Candace Hall
              Executive Editor
              Que Publishing
              800 East 96th Street
              Indianapolis, IN 46240 USA

For more information about this book or another Que Publishing title, visit our Web site at www.quepublishing.com. Type the ISBN (0789731797) or the title of a book in the Search field to find the page you're looking for.

Introduction

Remember *Monopoly*? I loved that game, and I was always the banker. I enjoyed stacking the money neatly in order by denomination, making sure the bills all faced the same way as they nestled in the little cardboard banker's drawer, and I kept the property cards in order according to their position on the board. (Yes, I was born to be an organizer.)

With an adult's perspective, it's interesting to recall my childhood approach to playing this game. I had a vague notion that you could borrow money, but I never did: In my *Monopoly* world, transactions were strictly cash-only. I didn't want to be bothered with keeping track of what I owed or gambling on whether I would have the payment in the future. I wanted to just hand the money over and be done with it, or, if I didn't have enough, to simply put the purchase out of my mind and roll the dice again.

As a grown-up I know that, no matter how much I wish it did, life doesn't work that way. Very few transactions happen in real time; almost everything, even a basic checking account, is based on credit, which adds layers of complexity to managing our money.

At the same time, credit has made life much more pleasant for millions of people, including me. Where would we live if we had to save up enough cash to buy a house without a mortgage? How safe could we possibly be if we had to carry around thousands of dollars in cash instead of one little card that's useless to a thief without the PIN? The credit system has been good to us, but it requires a heavy load of organization.

If you're like me, you see both the beauty and the impracticality of a simple cash system, and you sometimes resent the management that goes into the multiple bank accounts, credit cards, and investments of a typical family. Managing money is a necessary evil, not a hobby, so you want a system—a clear, concise, easy, and quick system—that allows you to track where your money is going, where it's coming from, and how much you actually have on any given day.

This has been a pet pursuit of mine since I got my first job back in high school, and over the years, I've tried a lot of things in my quest for the ideal financial management system. I've created highly detailed, complex, very accurate but very time-consuming processes, and I've tried the opposite extreme as well. With every new variation on my own methods, and with every system I've helped a client to develop for herself, I've learned something new about balancing the value of accuracy and detail with that of time and simplicity. I've learned the value of being "organized enough," and that's what I hope to convey to you with this book.

What *Organize Your Personal Finances In No Time* Can Do for You

The *In No Time* series was created for busy people who want to enhance areas of their lives that could use some organization. The title has two meanings: You want to get organized very quickly (seemingly in no time) and you need to accomplish this feat in the absence of spare time on your part (you have "no time" to organize). I know you don't want to make a career of this: You want to dive in, make improvements, and move on to the next project. So that's how you use this book—skim it, jump from chapter to chapter, take what you need, and go. You are, of course, welcome to read it cover to cover, savoring the author's wit and insight, but my feelings won't be hurt if you don't.

There are many fine books in print on general organizing and on managing your finances. This book bridges the gap between the two, showing you how to narrow the focus of foundational organizing techniques and direct them exclusively toward projects that clear the way for achievement of your financial goals.

Everything's easier when you're organized, and the best way to get there is one project at a time. You can organize the kitchen cabinets another day: For now, it's all about your money. Complete each of the projects in this book and you'll gain

- A foolproof system for collecting all of your receipts and ATM slips
- An income and expense tracking document and a technique for tracking cash expenditures on-the-fly

- The know-how to balance your checkbook by hand and information about options for setting up money management software
- A comprehensive bill-paying system that includes techniques for avoiding late fees and overdrafts
- An efficient method for managing incoming mail
- A comprehensive document storage and retrieval system, including paper and electronic files
- Techniques for creating a property inventory (both written and videotaped) and a plan for storing irreplaceable documents and computer media
- Tools to improve your efficiency as a consumer, including lists to prevent duplicate buying and a method for tracking items you've ordered
- Tools for calculating your net worth, debt-to-income ratio, and other personal statistics
- Resources for more information from experts on financial issues and advanced organizing

Along the way, you'll be able to see your finances from the perspective of a professional organizer, not a financial expert, so the focus stays on the efficiency of the system.

Who Should Read This Book?

If you believe that you could keep your finances organized with just a little direction and better systems, you've come to the right place. This book is meant for readers who

- Have moderately complicated personal finances (multiple accounts, investments, credit cards, insurance policies, and the like)
- Have recently experienced an event that made their finances more complicated (such as marriage, starting a business, or receiving an inheritance)
- Are take-charge types who want to be in control of their finances and want to manage the process themselves
- Enjoy being organized and are willing to put forth the effort to achieve that state
- Have had their finances managed by someone else in the past but now want to take over the job themselves
- Want to put new systems in place but don't want to create them from scratch

- Have financial problems, such as chronic bounced-check fees, that can be improved by organization
- Are already doing a pretty good job of keeping their finances organized but would like to make refinements

For some people, this book will be a great start, but it won't be the only help you need. If you are intimidated by organizing or have had little success with past organizing efforts, you might find it most beneficial to work through this book with the guidance of a professional organizer—preferably one with experience in chronic disorganization. If you have financial problems that organizing will not alleviate, such as serious debt or compulsive shopping, or if you have high anxiety over financial matters that causes you to avoid addressing money matters, you can learn valuable organizing skills from this book, but you also need to work with a financial expert or a counselor with expertise in your areas of additional need.

How This Book Is Organized

The lessons and projects in this book are presented in a logical sequence, so you will have a more seamless experience if you work through the book from beginning to end. However, if you prefer you can use portions of the book in random order—especially if you're already organized in some of these areas and simply want to fill in the gaps in your system.

This book is organized into three parts; here's what each contains:

- In Part I, "Capture the Numbers," you'll learn how to track every dollar as it comes and goes and finally see an accurate picture of your income and spending habits. You'll develop systems for ensuring nothing slips through the cracks, which will pave the way for you to balance your accounts and keep them balanced from here on out. After you've gotten a grip on the seemingly secret life of your money, you'll establish a proactive approach to bill-paying and put safeguards in place to prevent late fees and overdrafts. By the end of this section, you will have a fully functional process for capturing the data of your every deposit, check, debit, and withdrawal.
- In Part II, "Corral the Paper," we set our sights on taming all of the statements, letters, bills, and other documents that enter your life (often uninvited). You'll establish some ruthless rules for managing the mail, and you'll find yourself throwing away much more than you have in the past. For the lucky papers that get to stay, you'll create a streamlined, easy-to-use filing system—or perhaps a legitimate "piling" system instead. You'll put special safeguards in place for your most critical documents, and you'll finally get those stacks of paper off your desk (or floor) and therefore off your mind!

- In Part III, "Advanced Projects," you get to have some fun. You'll learn some impressive organizing tricks that you can show off to your friends, all while taking your efficiency to new heights. Here you'll find organizing tools to get shopping down to a science and ways to make your planner (paper or electronic) work harder for you. Also in this section, if you want to tinker with the financial numbers you now have at your fingertips, you'll find formulas for calculating your net worth, your debt-to-income ratio, and even your own personal profit-and-loss statement. If you want to create a savings or debt repayment plan, you can do it with the tools in this section. Appendix A contains a list of useful references and resources, and you'll find blank copies of the spreadsheets used in this book in Appendix B.

Special Elements and Icons

Throughout this book, you'll find a variety of special elements—lists, sidebars, icons, and other "extras" designed to catch your eye and call out items of special interest relevant to the nearby text. Some of these special elements are described here to help you learn how to use their information when you encounter them in your reading.

To-Do and You'll Need Lists

Each chapter of the book includes a list of what you'll need and one or more to-do lists. You'll Need gives you a quick reference for shopping: Be sure you have these items on hand before you begin so you can make the most of your organizing time. The items on your To-Do Lists give you the steps you'll take to complete the projects in each section.

Basic Organizing Principles

There are a few organizing principles that I think of as the foundations of what I do as a professional organizer. One or more of these principles comes into play with every job I take, and each of my clients becomes accustomed to hearing me mention them again and again. Because these ideas are so important, I've flagged examples of them throughout the book with the icons you see here. Absorb these key principles into your approach to organizing your finances, then use them in other areas of your life and see what a difference they'll make for you:

Have a Home: Designate a *home* for every item you own, including all types of paper. A major component of clutter management is knowing where to put things when you're ready to put them away. Not everything has to be in its home all the time, just as long as it has a space reserved for it and can go there anytime.

Be Consistent: Do things the same way each time. Invest in creating a method that you can easily develop into productive habits, and avoid reinventing the wheel each time. This is especially important in managing your finances and documents because many intertwined subsystems are at work and you can easily lose track of what you're trying to do and how you meant to do it.

Use Your System: A system works only if you apply it comprehensively and consistently. If the process isn't working, modify it to meet your needs or even switch to something completely different, but don't abandon the project altogether. Being organized will always require some effort on your part, but it should be like a merry-go-round: You have to pull hard and run with it to get it going, but once it has momentum, you can just stand still and give it a regularly scheduled push.

Organized Enough: Be only as organized as you have to be. Avoid organizing for its own sake. Organizing is not something that has inherent value, like kindness, for example. Kindness is a good thing to practice even if it provides no direct benefit for you. Organizing, on the other hand, is a tool that should be used only for a reason: Organize your paperwork to save yourself time and frustration in the future, not just to put it in a different order. If it's alphabetized A to Z, don't make it Z to A just because. When you're organized enough, stop.

Clever Client: These are solutions that my clients have discovered on their own, usually through hard-fought trial and error. Most of my clients have AD/HD (attention deficit/hyperactivity disorder), so they've had to find ways to compensate for what they lack in attentiveness, impulse control, or planning ability. They love sharing their tips because they get to help others and at the same time prove that they're not, as the famous AD/HD book title says, "lazy, stupid, or crazy." Best of all, these little gems are often better than anything a non-AD/HD organizer could dream up!

Finding "the" Way

"This is my way. What is your way? THE way does not exist." —Friedrich Nietzsche

A final point before we dive into your financial life: In organizing, as in life, there is always more than one right way. This can be frustrating if you're tired of trying to choose and simply want someone to show you the way so you can embrace it without second-guessing. In this book, I present you with just one or a few options—the ones I have found to be the most useful, easy, or popular with my clients—and invite you to apply all of my techniques as-is or to modify them as you wish. I encourage you to find your own ideal balance between the time invested and the usefulness of the end result—your unique version of "organized enough."

Part 1

Capture the Numbers

1   Tracking Your Money 9

2   Getting the Figures to Match 29

3   Avoiding Late Fees and Overdrafts 47

Tracking Your Money

If you're like many of my clients, you feel the need to keep track of your earnings and spending. You want to ensure that your accounts are balanced and your bills are paid, and that nothing is overlooked. As an adult, managing your money properly is the responsible thing to do. If you don't feel you're doing it right, money management can become a source of anxiety and embarrassment, and eventually you might become so intimidated by the whole process that you avoid dealing with it altogether. You don't want to do that, of course, because that would compound the problem pretty quickly.

Instead, take advantage of the tools and encouragement I offer you in this chapter. You'll begin by getting your mind around the task ahead and then jump right into solving the problem of misplaced receipts, forgotten ATM slips, and other unrecorded expenditures that lead to those infuriating overdraft fees. From there, you'll create a document to record all of those expenditures after you've captured them. And finally, you'll learn how to navigate the sometimes tricky waters of managing joint accounts, so your new system isn't thwarted by a partner who forgets to tell you about his or her spending.

By the time you've finished the projects in this chapter, you'll have a comprehensive system for recording every bit of income and expenditures for yourself and anyone else who shares accounts with you, and you'll feel a whole lot more organized.

In this chapter:

* Considering the task ahead
* Finding the right system
* Snaring every piece of information
* Creating a tracking document
* Tracking for two: managing joint accounts

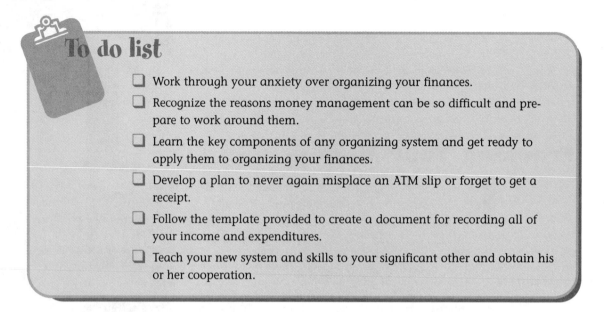

To do list

- ☐ Work through your anxiety over organizing your finances.
- ☐ Recognize the reasons money management can be so difficult and prepare to work around them.
- ☐ Learn the key components of any organizing system and get ready to apply them to organizing your finances.
- ☐ Develop a plan to never again misplace an ATM slip or forget to get a receipt.
- ☐ Follow the template provided to create a document for recording all of your income and expenditures.
- ☐ Teach your new system and skills to your significant other and obtain his or her cooperation.

Getting Your Mind Around the Task Ahead

You have in your hands an entire book of projects for organizing your finances, and you want to complete them in as little time and with as little stress as possible. To do that, you must let go of any lingering fear, doubt, or self-recrimination you might be harboring about your abilities in this area. First, stop blaming yourself if you have trouble getting a mental grip on financial management. The truth is it's not easy; financial management is complex, and it takes time, precision, and a lot of attention to detail. Even if you're highly skilled in other areas, organizing and managing finances might be challenging for you—that's probably why you purchased this book! To get the most from the advice offered here, though, you need to disregard your past failures and commit fully to creating your own solution using the tools, systems, and ideas contained here.

It's really no wonder that so many highly intelligent, fully functional people feel that getting a grip on their money is like trying to nail Jell-O to the wall. The next time you're feeling like a failure for not fully comprehending our modern-day money system, consider these facts about money today:

- **Money is invisible**—"Yeah, no kidding money is invisible," you're thinking. "Mine vanishes all the time!" That might be true as well, but what I mean is that we never actually see or touch most of our money. You could earn $50,000 a year and handle only $1,040 of it—$20 a week—in actual cash.

Our banking systems are so fully automated now, with electronic payment methods becoming the norm even at fast-food drive-thrus, that carrying more than $100 cash can feel unnecessary and maybe even dangerous.

- **Money time-travels**—It's startling to realize how much of your money doesn't actually exist at a given moment. Consider the basic checking account. It seems like a repository for your cash, but that checking account is actually a short-term line of credit. The bank holds your money and lets you write permission slips for other people to come in and take some of it. So that money is committed to someone in the future, but for now it's still there. When you deposit a check, the bank might put a hold on it until it can confirm the money will actually come through. So, it might seem that you have the money in your account now, but in reality that money exists for someone else a few days in the past, and it won't be yours until a few days into the future. Mind-boggling, yes? Add in the phenomena of the ATM transaction that clears in 3 days, the 30-day revolving credit card account, and the 30-year mortgage, and you just might find yourself yearning for the old cash-under-the-mattress system.

If you're still feeling self-critical, don't worry. You'll lose the guilt once you've completed the projects in this chapter. Now, let's get started.

You'll need list

- ☐ Paper and pencil and/or your computer
- ☐ A case or container for your receipts
- ☐ Bills to be paid
- ☐ A calendar

Arming Yourself with the Right Organization System

There are hundreds of "right" ways to organize anything, whether you're trying to apply order to your finances, your garage, or your clothes closet, but every successful system has a few things in common:

- **Comprehensiveness**—The system covers the common components of the area it is addressing (for finances, that would be checking accounts and credit cards), but it can also accommodate not-so-obvious components (such as cash spending).
- **Simplicity**—The system is no more complex than it has to be.
- **Appropriateness**—The system is a good fit for the user's skills, patience, and available time.
- **Flexibility**—The system can be changed as needed when life changes come along.

A good organizing system has quite a lot to live up to. In contrast, you have just one duty: Consistency. No system, no matter how perfect, will work if you don't use it. The system has to do most of the work, but you have to create it and follow it for it to perform for you.

With that in mind, let's get started on your first project: a method for keeping transactions from slipping through the cracks.

To do list

- ☐ Set up a foolproof system for retaining all receipts and ATM slips.
- ☐ Make provisions for recording transactions with no receipt.
- ☐ Practice the new habits you'll need to develop to make your system work for you.
- ☐ Choose one place to collect your various receipts until it's time to enter them into the income and expense spreadsheet you'll create in the next section.

Building a Fence to Snare Every Last Scrap of Your Financial Information

What a relief it will be! Soon you'll have a reliable method for holding onto a record of every transaction long enough to get it into the tracking document you'll create in the next section.

Here's a problem that our prehistoric ancestors could relate to. Say you're a shepherd like the one in Figure 1.1. It's getting to be dinner time, you're anxious to get home and put your feet up in front of the fire, and you look over your flock and think, "Am I missing one?"

FIGURE 1.1

Your great-great-great-great-uncle the shepherd probably worried about losing track of his sheep the way you worry about wayward receipts.

Millions of years later, we get that same sinking feeling about our wayward receipts, check carbons, and ATM slips: the modern-day herd we each must tend. As sheep are notorious for wandering off to explore little outcroppings halfway down a cliff, our gasoline receipts seem to have the same fascination with that knuckle-scraping gap between the car seats. They say paper comes from trees, but behaviorally it has more in common with livestock.

So, how can you keep your flock from straying? Build an escape-proof fence in the form of a receipt-collection system that covers every possible scenario.

Your mission is to capture and hold a record of every single transaction you make until you're ready to process them. Your fence, so to speak, will be the collection of methods you use to make sure none of these rascals gets by you.

Changing Habits

Congratulations, you're already halfway there! Awareness of the need for change is half the battle. Now extend that awareness to attentiveness of your day-to-day behavior. Consider these questions as you prepare to build your fence:

- **What types of transactions do I have?**—Is it mostly bank-card purchases? What about ATM or drive-thru withdrawals or deposits? How often do you spend cash?

- **What do I usually do with receipts?**—Do you stuff them in your pocket or purse, throw them in the shopping bag, or stash them in your car visor or up on the dashboard? If you had to find a particular receipt, what are all the places you might think to look?

- **What do I *think* I should be doing with receipts?**—Is there a bowl or in-box that you always intend to collect your receipts in (even though that doesn't always happen)? Keep this spot in mind: It will probably become the center of your receipt-collection plan—the corral around which your fence is built.

- **What do I always seem to lose?**—You probably have at least one type of transaction that often gets lost. Think about why that happens. Is there something about this transaction that makes saving the record or properly storing the receipt inconvenient? My "problem sheep" are pay-at-the-pump gas receipts (I'm in a hurry, it's cold out, and I stuff the receipt in my pocket instead of my wallet) and Amazon.com purchases (I don't always remember to print out the onscreen receipt). Figure out which items seem to fall through the cracks and why, and you can mend a big hole in the receipt-corral fence.

- **What if I don't get a receipt?**—What happens if you write a check or use your bank card and for some reason they can't give you a receipt? Do you have a backup plan for capturing that transaction? (Check out the section "Tracking Cash, With or Without Receipts," later in this chapter, for more on this dilemma.) This is another reason that pay-at-the-pump gas receipts are a problem for me: Sometimes the receipt printer is out of paper, and if I had time to go inside and get a copy, I wouldn't have paid at the pump in the first place!

Pay attention to what you do every time you handle money. Do you get a receipt or make a record of every transaction? If not, what gets in your way? What can you change to eliminate these obstacles? What can you do as a last resort if your regular system doesn't work, and how can you trigger yourself to engage that last resort?

When you observe yourself in a variety of transaction situations, you'll begin to recognize the ones that wreak havoc with your money management. Practice compensating for these with some sort of workaround. For example, if I'm tempted to grab that gas receipt and run, I ask myself why: Am I freezing? Fine, get in the car, start it, and take a second to put the receipt where it belongs. Was the stupid printer out of paper? Scribble the date, amount, and card used on a scrap of something, even a blank space on another receipt already in my wallet. Am I in a hurry to drive away because some shady character is lurking nearby? Okay, engage the last-resort receipt-handling plan: Get in and go, but keep the receipt or a scrap of paper to make one in my hand until I get to a red light or my destination; then put it where it belongs.

With the Amazon.com purchase problem, I added a new behavior to try to reinforce the one I'm supposed to be doing. Since I couldn't rely on myself to always print out the receipt and put it in the container until the next day I balance my accounts, now I open QuickBooks as I'm finishing the Amazon transaction—right at the point where I'm smiling and thinking, "Cool! I should have that book in about two days!"—and I key in the purchase right then and there (see Figure 1.2).

tip The back of an ATM slip makes a great do-it-yourself receipt. Use that space to record cash expenditures and purchases for which you weren't given a receipt. Note the date, store, amount, and how you paid. Add an arrow on the front of the slip to remind yourself to also look at the back when recording transactions later.

FIGURE 1.2

I'm inclined to make impulse purchases on Amazon.com and forget to print out the receipt, so I enter the transaction in QuickBooks as soon as I complete the purchase.

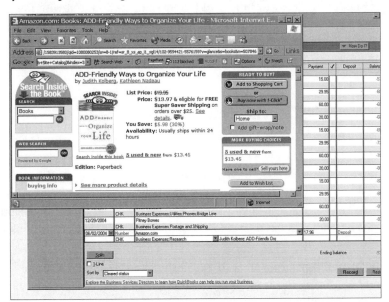

You, too, can build a set of adaptive processes like these. Instead of chastising yourself for losing receipts or forgetting transactions, just think, "Okay, so this is a glitch for me, but it doesn't make me a bad person. Now how can I solve this problem?" The best solutions anticipate our quirky humanness and help us to work around it.

Choosing the Gathering Place

After you've learned how to herd every last transaction and get it moving in the right direction, you need to have a destination ready to receive and keep those transactions. There's that ancient behavior again: You can get sheep to come home, but once they do, they need a place to stay.

This destination spot can be anything that is large enough to hold receipts of any size, protected from breezes or pets that might steal your captives away again, and convenient enough that you'll actually use it. Mine is a zippered compartment of my wallet; I've trained myself to put receipts there no matter what. When I'm ready to reconcile my accounts, I retrieve all of my receipts from this spot and key them in to QuickBooks. You have dozens of options besides your wallet: a container in your closet, bathroom, or kitchen (wherever you empty your pockets each day); a zippered bag in your car or purse (anything from a lovely leather case to a simple sandwich bag); or a binder clip used like a money clip to keep them all together. Try any idea that appeals to you, and if it doesn't work, try another!

It's not always easy to snare every single transaction, but with my various ways of making sure I get a receipt and herding it into the holding spot, there aren't very many situations that my system can't handle. This should be your goal as well: Improve your system until you become as close to perfect as any modern-day shepherd can be.

Tracking Cash, With or Without Receipts

There is one thing that can throw a wrench into any expense-tracking system quicker than you can say "miscellaneous": the ATM cash advance.

You can be ultra-disciplined about recording check and credit card purchases, collecting all of your receipts to enter into your system, and categorizing your expenditures so you can see where your money is going, but that cash advance receipt can create a big question mark: You know you took $20 out of the bank, but what did you do with it?

If you don't spend much cash and cash advances don't add up to a significant amount for you each month, you can probably skip this section. If you do want to close this gap, here are some improvements you can make to your system to accommodate cash spending:

- Ask for receipts for absolutely everything, even fast food. Keep these receipts with all the others you'll be recording in your system.

- If a receipt is not available for a cash purchase (or if you feel silly asking for one at McDonald's), use the ATM slip from the original cash advance to keep a tally of what you spend it on. If you take out $20, on the back of the ATM slip, jot down where and when you spend that $20.

- If you use money management software, create an account called Cash, similar to the checking, savings, and credit card accounts already in the system. Record your cash spending here and categorize each expense the same as you would in your other accounts.

If you maintain a Cash account record in your money management program, you don't have to maintain an accurate balance for this account if you don't want to.

For some people, "cash" is itself enough of an explanation; they don't feel the need to know what that cash was spent on. For others, particularly those trying to stick to a budget, it's imperative to know exactly where every penny goes. Determine your needs based on your unique situation and categorize in only as much detail as you need. Just remember whether you're tracking cash partially or fully and whether or not the balance in your Cash account is accurate when you run reports.

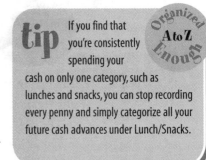

tip If you find that you're consistently spending your cash on only one category, such as lunches and snacks, you can stop recording every penny and simply categorize all your future cash advances under Lunch/Snacks.

Recording Every Transaction, Even When You're Rushed

You've unloaded your cart at the grocery store, and now you're impatiently waiting for the customer ahead of you to get out of the way. You want to move forward and check the prices on the screen as the cashier scans in your items, and the bagger needs your cart, but this slowpoke is fumbling with bags, receipts, gloves, and kids, and you're trapped.

Minutes later, you're the one finishing your transaction and gathering your things to go. You sure don't want to be The Slowpoke, so you swoop everything into one hand and hurry out of the way. I call this "doing the Next-in-Line Hustle."

Days later, you're pulling your hair out, trying to balance your checkbook and filling in missing transactions from memory. You vow that, from now on, you will write down every purchase as it happens. And you mean it this time. Really.

Every organizing system, no matter how good, can break down when we're rushed. What's the key to making any system work? Actually following it. And what gets in the way of following it? Not taking the time to do it correctly and completely. Your goal is to capture every transaction, so you need a technique that is lightning-fast and fits every situation.

Keeping Track when Paying with a Card

I prefer paying by card instead of by check because I usually get just one receipt that tells me everything I need to know: what I bought, how much I spent, the date, and the account I paid with. Here's how I do the Next-in-Line Hustle, Card Version:

1. Hand over the card or run it through the machine myself.
2. Sign the screen or paper copy.
3. Grab the card, receipt, and ribbon of coupons and stuff them all into the back section of my wallet.
4. Zip up my wallet (see Figure 1.3), grab my bags, and dash.
5. Repeat all week.
6. Take the bulging wallet to my desk, pull out the wad of receipts and check carbons, open QuickBooks, and key in the week's purchases.

FIGURE 1.3
I use this zippered leather case to hold my wallet contents and my PDA. This is all I need to hit the mall or grocery store and keep my receipts and ATM slips organized.

Keeping Track when Paying by Check

Even though I prefer using a card, sometimes I have to write a check. I use duplicate checks (the kind with a piece of carbon paper attached), so I know the check number and who it was written to without having to record the transaction in a check register. Here's my Next-in-Line Hustle, Check Version:

1. Pull out the book of checks and tear one off.
2. Fill out the check, separate it from the carbon, and hand it over.
3. Put away the unused checks, my pen, and the check carbon while I wait for the receipt.
4. Pop the receipt into the back section of the wallet with the check carbon.
5. Zip, grab bags, dash.
6. Repeat.
7. QuickBooks.

> **tip**
> If you want to pay with a card but the machine won't read it, wrap a piece of plastic around the card and run it through. Even an opaque grocery bag will do. This trick will buy you some time until you can get your worn-out card replaced.

Did you notice that I don't use a check register? ("Gasp! She doesn't write it all down line by line???") Nope, I don't need to. I get a receipt for every transaction and keep the check carbon for every check I write, so each weekend when I update my QuickBooks records, I enter everything, balance my checking account, and start every Monday knowing just how much of an allowance I have for the week.

Did you also notice that this doesn't sound like an especially neat-looking method? You're right, it's not. By the end of the week, it's a jumble of wrinkly little slips of paper. But nonetheless, it never fails me. (Except when my friend Cindy dumps my wallet on the floor and the receipts slide under her stove. But that was my fault for leaving it unzipped.)

Why does this always work? Because I do the *same thing every time*. If I deviate from this routine, I get little surprises on my account statement. When my statement shows me that I have less money than I think I have, I'm once again reminded that deviating from my system is more trouble than it's worth.

To do list

- ☐ Determine the line items that will be included in your spreadsheet, including all sources of income and all expenses.
- ☐ Choose whether to create your spreadsheet on paper or using your computer.
- ☐ Set up the rows and columns of your spreadsheet.
- ☐ Enter lines for sources of income.
- ☐ Carefully choose your expense categories and enter them into your spreadsheet.
- ☐ Fill in income and expense data.

Creating an Income and Expense Tracking Document

Okay, you've got all of your receipts. Now what do you do with them?

Even if you use software such as Quicken by Intuit or Microsoft Money (covered in more detail in Chapter 2, "Getting the Figures to Match"), you might find it helpful to keep a separate income and expense tracking document. You can run reports in your money management program that show you how you're doing with your financial goals, but the act of hand-writing or keying in the figures in a separate document can help you see the big picture more easily. I use QuickBooks (the business version of Quicken) to record all my transactions and balance all of my accounts electronically, but I also use another spreadsheet to list all of the data I want to see together, not all of which has a place in QuickBooks where it can be entered. I've tried to create just the right custom report in QuickBooks to eliminate the need for this spreadsheet, but so far nothing has worked as well as my trusty Excel document.

You can create your spreadsheet by hand on graph paper, in a ledger book purchased from an office supply store, or on the computer using a database program such as Microsoft Excel or Access (or even a word-processing program that allows you to create tables, such as Microsoft Word). A database program has the capability to perform calculations for you—a time-saving advantage if you know the program well enough to set the formulas.

You'll need list

☐ Either paper and a pen or pencil (for a hand-drawn spreadsheet) or software (Excel, another database program, or a word-processing program) for a computer-based spreadsheet.

☐ The receipts you collected in the previous section.

Laying the Foundation

There are a few components your spreadsheet will need to have, no matter how you create it. These are

- An Income section and an Expenses section
- Categories for subdividing expenses, and also for income if you receive payments from more than one source

- Regularly recurring time increments, whether monthly, weekly, or quarterly
- Spaces for both anticipated and actual amounts
- Spaces for total income and total expenses by time period

Figure 1.4 is an example of an income and expense tracking document that incorporates all these elements in a space-efficient manner. I created this one in Microsoft Excel, my first choice because I can change it at will, insert or delete lines, attach embedded notes to each field, and have the program automatically perform calculations for me. I can also make the spreadsheet as large as I want because I work on the computer, not on a printout that's limited by the size of the paper.

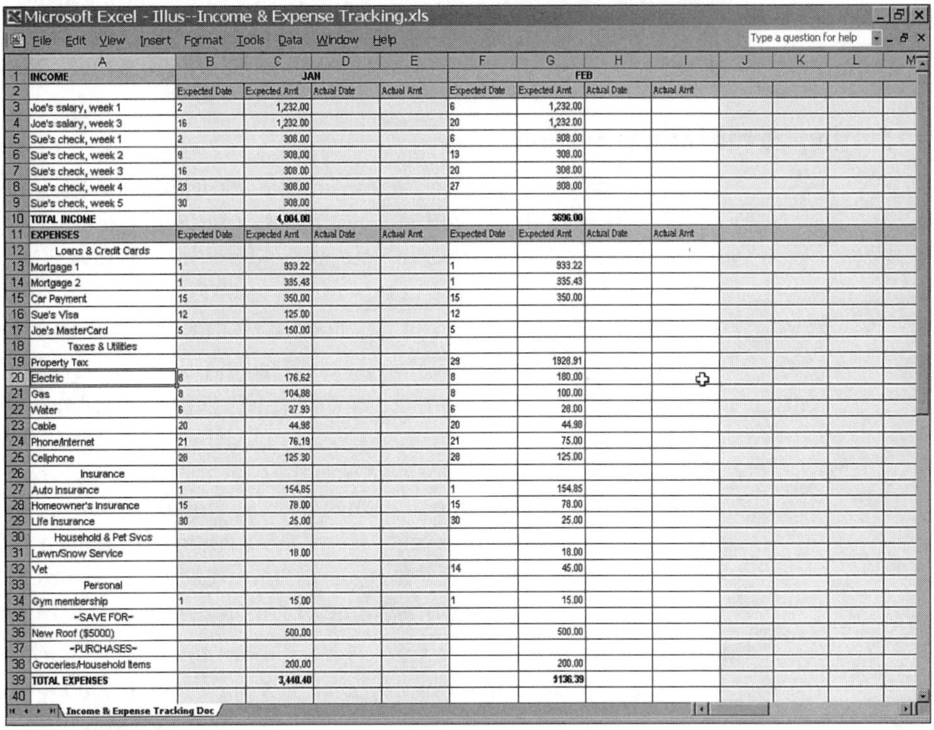

	A	B	C	D	E	F	G	H	I
1	INCOME	JAN				FEB			
2		Expected Date	Expected Amt	Actual Date	Actual Amt	Expected Date	Expected Amt	Actual Date	Actual Amt
3	Joe's salary, week 1	2	1,232.00			6	1,232.00		
4	Joe's salary, week 3	16	1,232.00			20	1,232.00		
5	Sue's check, week 1	2	308.00			6	308.00		
6	Sue's check, week 2	9	308.00			13	308.00		
7	Sue's check, week 3	16	308.00			20	308.00		
8	Sue's check, week 4	23	308.00			27	308.00		
9	Sue's check, week 5	30	308.00						
10	TOTAL INCOME		4,004.00				3696.00		
11	EXPENSES	Expected Date	Expected Amt	Actual Date	Actual Amt	Expected Date	Expected Amt	Actual Date	Actual Amt
12	Loans & Credit Cards								
13	Mortgage 1	1	933.22			1	933.22		
14	Mortgage 2	1	335.43			1	335.43		
15	Car Payment	15	350.00			15	350.00		
16	Sue's Visa	12	125.00			12			
17	Joe's MasterCard	5	150.00			5			
18	Taxes & Utilities								
19	Property Tax					29	1928.91		
20	Electric	8	176.62			8	180.00		
21	Gas	8	104.88			8	100.00		
22	Water	6	27.93			6	28.00		
23	Cable	20	44.98			20	44.98		
24	Phone/Internet	21	76.19			21	75.00		
25	Cellphone	28	125.30			28	125.00		
26	Insurance								
27	Auto Insurance	1	154.85			1	154.85		
28	Homeowner's Insurance	15	78.00			15	78.00		
29	Life Insurance	30	25.00			30	25.00		
30	Household & Pet Svcs								
31	Lawn/Snow Service		18.00				18.00		
32	Vet					14	45.00		
33	Personal								
34	Gym membership	1	15.00			1	15.00		
35	~SAVE FOR~								
36	New Roof ($5000)		500.00				500.00		
37	~PURCHASES~								
38	Groceries/Household Items		200.00				200.00		
39	TOTAL EXPENSES		3,440.40				5136.39		
40									

FIGURE 1.4
Refer to this example of an income and expense tracking spreadsheet as you complete the steps of this section. This computerized spreadsheet was created in Microsoft Excel.

Choosing Your Time Increments

When you set up your tracking document, you will need to decide whether you will measure time in months, weeks, quarters, or another increment. Because most recurring bills are paid on a monthly basis, it makes sense to use one-month increments in your tracking document. For items that are paid less frequently (for example, if your water bill is quarterly), you can simply enter them in the months they are paid and leave the other months blank.

Choosing Your Page Size

A complete tracking document for an entire year will have 49 columns (1 column to list income sources and expense categories, followed by 4 columns for each month) and enough rows to list all your income, expenses, and totals. If you're using pencil and paper or a word-processing program, you can list 1–3 months per page; in an electronic spreadsheet program, you can list the entire year in one document.

Creating the Header Row and Category Column

In the top row of your tracking document, skip the first column and then divide the remaining 48 columns into groups of 4. You will use these 4 columns for each month: Expected Date, Expected Amount, Actual Date, and Actual Amount. These columns will serve slightly different purposes in the income and expense sections, so create them all, even if you feel you don't need all 4 in one of the sections.

Setting Up the Income Section

When setting up the Income section, consult a calendar to determine how many weeks or pay periods will fall in each month; then make a line for each payment you will receive. For example, if you are paid on the first and third Friday of each month, you'll have two lines per month to record your income. If you are paid every Friday, however, the number of pay periods changes from month to month.

If you are self-employed or your pay is project-based, you're probably rolling your eyes and thinking, "I *can't* project my income!" Believe me, I feel your pain. You might not be able to plug in a salary figure for the next 12 months, but you can anticipate at least a short distance into the future. Projecting income is one of the inherent challenges of being your own boss. Laying out your projected income for an entire year won't be an option for you, but anticipating even just a month or two ahead and monitoring how close your Estimated Amount comes to matching your Actual Amount will make your financial life more predictable and less scary.

Make a line for each project you are hired for at the time you accept it and enter the amount it will pay in the month you expect to receive that payment. Don't worry about getting the amount exactly right: Remember that you have a column for Estimated Amount (your best guess right now) and another column for Actual Amount (the amount you enter when you have the payment in hand).

In the Expected Date column for each month, record the date on which you anticipate receiving a payment. If you have a regularly recurring salary or your company issues paychecks on the same day each week, this will be easy: Just consult the calendar. If your pay is project-based, use your judgment and past experience with each client to determine a reasonable date to expect payment—for example, 30 days after invoicing.

In the Expected Amount column, record the payment you anticipate. Again, if you are paid by salary, this will be simple. If you are hourly and work a varying number of hours each week, enter an average amount based on your recent work schedules; then update the figure when you receive your schedule for the upcoming pay period. For project work, enter the amount you will be billing for each project.

> **tip**
>
> If you're self-employed, filling in the estimated and actual figures for every project can help you improve your financial planning skills over time. You might make some useful observations: Do you tend to overestimate your pay? Do some projects tend to pay late most of the time? Use these discoveries to refine your marketing and billing practices and to be more discerning in which clients you choose to work with.

In the Actual Date and Actual Amount columns, record the actual figures when they occur. Seeing the estimated versus actual dates and amounts will be informative in the future: You'll be able to see how well you estimate and how predictable your income actually is.

Setting Up the Expenses Section

For most people, income doesn't need to be subdivided into categories because it comes from only one source. If you receive income from several sources and want to track each of them, you simply create a line for each in the Income section. If you share your finances with someone else, record his or her income in the same way.

However, detailed expense categories are important for everyone: This action allows you to see more clearly where your money is going, which makes this document very illuminating if you need to tighten your budget.

It's important to put some thought into these categories upfront. If you use money management software, you might have already done this; if so, be consistent and use the same categories in this spreadsheet. If not, you'll create categories now that you can later replicate in Quicken or Money if you choose to use software.

Categorizing Expenses

There are many metaphors and technical terms to describe the process of categorizing and subcategorizing data. Some people picture a set of nesting dolls—the ones that open at the middle to reveal a smaller doll inside. Others picture the branches of a tree, with the trunk representing the entire set, the main limbs as the broad categories, and the smaller branches as the subcategories. Some think of it as resembling an outline or a set of steps. For some, the term *concatenation* or *chart of accounts* says it all. Use whatever terminology or mental imagery works for you.

In Figure 1.4 you saw just a few basic expense categories and subcategories. You can have as many levels of subcategorization as you want, but keep in mind that the more detailed your system is, the more work it will be to maintain it and the harder it will be to remember what you were doing if you're away from it for a few days or weeks. Try to choose a level of detail that provides just as much information as you need and no more.

For example, take utility bills. You could use one category for all of them: Have one line labeled Utilities and group all payments for electricity, gas, water, and so on into that single category. Or you could have separate lines for each. Can you think of a reason that you might need to see those figures separately and wouldn't want to pull out the bills to check them? If yes, list them separately; if no, keep it simple and go with the single, general category.

The last section of categories you should include in your expense-tracking document is Purchases. Purchases are distinct from Bills in that the expense occurs when you go out and spend money; it's not a bill representing a financial commitment you've already made. You can include this section if you want to track all of your spending in this spreadsheet, or you can use this sheet just for bills.

Don't worry about making your Expense categories perfect: You can always make changes later. Remember, every good organizing system must have the capacity to change with your needs—you're not wedded to it for life. You can add, delete, or change categories and subcategories whenever you want or need to.

tip If you're having trouble deciding which of two things should be the main category and which should be the subcategory, for example Insurance versus Auto Expenses, ask yourself which category is "bigger" to you. Would you make the Auto Insurance file a subset of Auto, or would you make Auto Insurance a subset of Insurance? In other words, would it make more sense to group all insurances together with subcategories of Auto, Health, Life, and Homeowner's, or to group all auto expenses together with subcategories including Insurance and Maintenance? Figure out which is the "bigger" or main category in your mind, and therefore which should be its subcategories.

Recording the Expected Dates and Amounts of Expenses

You have several options for how you will handle the Expected Date column in the Expenses section. No matter which option you choose, the most important thing is to apply it consistently. You can use the Expected Date column to note the following:

- **The date each bill is due**—This is usually the most informative data for this column.

- **The date you expect to receive each bill**—If you pay your bills as soon as they arrive, this might be the most useful date to record.

- **The date you intend to pay each bill**—If you don't pay each bill upon receipt but you want to be prompted to pay it a few days before it's due, or if you have some bills you intentionally pay after the due date but within the grace period, such as a mortgage or property taxes, this might be the best option for you. If this date will fall outside the month you're listing the item in, be sure to include the month (not just the day) in this field.

In the Expected Amount column, record the amount you intend to pay. Again, you have several options:

- **The actual amount due**—This is simply the amount you're being billed for.

- **More than the amount due**—If you pay more than the minimum toward your mortgage or credit cards, you can record an amount larger than what's actually owed for this billing cycle.

- **Less than the amount due**—If you're facing a month of more expenses than income, you can use this column to plan which bills will receive partial payment.

In the Actual Date and Actual Amount columns, record the actual figures when they occur.

Seeing the Big Picture

After you've filled in all of your categories and data, total your expected income and expenses and—deep breath—see which is greater. This is your spreadsheet's reason for being, and it's also the most gut-wrenching part of the whole process. As you can see in Figure 1.4, Sue and Joe's expenses were much less than their income in January, but February is going to present a problem....

Congratulations! You've completed a major step toward organizing your finances. Now maintain this spreadsheet as you continue with the rest of the projects in this book, and keep refining it as you move into your increasingly organized future.

But what if you're not the only one manipulating the money in your accounts? Here's your final project for this chapter: learning to cooperate with your joint-account partners.

Managing Joint Accounts: A Five-Point Peace Plan

It's unlikely that you and your significant other agree on everything. If you share one or more bank accounts, however, you're going to have to agree on some things if you ever hope to have your finances in order.

Perhaps you have different views on money. Maybe one of you is a saver (also known as penny-pincher, cheapskate, tightwad) and the other is a spender (also known as irresponsible, impulsive, materialistic). (If you're calling each other these parenthetical names, consider it a red flag.) Perhaps one is better at the day-to-day details of managing the account. Maybe neither of you is especially great at recording every transaction and a search would reveal ATM slips under the seats of both of your cars.

GETTING THE AID OF A FINANCIAL ADVISOR

If you're at each other's throats about money, applying the ideas in this book might help you to reach a truce, but it's likely that your bruised feelings will make the process much more difficult. Money—lack of it, use of it, even an excess of it—brings out primal fears and defense mechanisms in even the most easygoing folks, but there are ways to find common ground. If you can't agree on the following five points, make an investment in your relationship by enlisting the help of an expert—a counselor, therapist, clergy member, or financial advisor—who is experienced in helping couples see eye-to-eye about money (see Appendix A, "Further Reading and References," for sources of further information and assistance).

No matter how you feel about the big issues like saving for the future, investing, or how much your home or vehicles should cost, if you want to commingle your finances, you're going to have to agree on these points:

1. **One of you is the account manager, and the other is not**—It is nearly impossible for two people to take equal responsibility for managing the family finances. Decide which of you will be the account manager for your family. Who should it be? Some couples believe it should be the person who has more time, and some believe it should be the husband because handling the money is "the man's job." Neither of these criteria is valid. People who are

detail-oriented, able to remain emotionally uninvolved, and fairly tolerant of repetitive tasks tend to be better suited to money management—and those qualities are found in both men and women, and in both really busy and less-busy folks. Set aside your pride, society's gender norms, and all your other time commitments and decide which of you should be the account manager based on one criterion: Which of you is better at this?

After you've decided whose responsibility this will be, give that person room to work. The account manager needs his or her partner to step back, have faith, and not second-guess the system.

2. **Being the account manager does not make you the boss of the other**—Don't gloat. Yes, you're the account manager because you're better at this stuff than your partner. When you start to feel smug, remind yourself of three things you're hopeless at that your partner can do with ease. Remind yourself, because if you don't, your partner will.

   Don't "parent." Handling the family finances is your job, but it doesn't make you superior to your partner. When you inform your partner of where you stand financially each time you balance your accounts, don't make it a lecture. When you tell your partner how much money is available for discretionary spending, don't call it an allowance. If your partner made errors—forgot to tell you about a purchase or ATM withdrawal or spent more than the budgeted amount—relate the errors in a neutral tone and be sure to relate any errors you made as well. You're summarizing account activity, not laying blame.

   Don't joke with friends about which of you controls the purse strings. You're both in charge of the money; you share the big decisions. As a team, one of you tracks the details and keeps the other informed. You're equals. Resist becoming drunk on your imagined power.

3. **The account manager communicates fully with the other financial partner**—Aside from the responsibility to manage the accounts accurately, you are also responsible for keeping your partner fully informed. It's not fair to use your partner's distance from the details against him. Don't hide transactions. Don't use your role as an opportunity to make financial decisions that you know he would not agree to.

4. **You both adhere to your established system**—Points 1–3 address the behavior and attitude of the account manager, but this point applies more to the other partner.

   For any system to work, it must be followed completely and consistently. For the account manager to do a good job, both of you must follow the system.

Don't make the account manager track you down for receipts or extra information on deposits or expenditures. Don't withdraw more cash than you've agreed to. Don't pretend that you don't understand the system—if you don't, then you both need to sit down and clarify it. Don't keep saying "I forgot" or "But I needed it." If you don't give the account manager the necessary information and cooperation, you'll make it impossible for your partner to continue treating you like a responsible adult.

5. **If the system needs refinement, work together to make changes**— Every organizing system will need to evolve to accommodate the changes life brings. If you find that a component of your financial system is causing problems for one of you, you must both be willing to find a resolution, even if it means one of you gives something up or accepts a new inconvenience. If one of you is unable to remember every expenditure, find a way to minimize the damage—for example, by limiting which accounts you spend from or giving up your ATM card. If you've agreed that you will both empty your wallets, pockets, and car consoles of receipts every day and deposit them in a designated spot, but one of you sometimes forgets, consider other options: Could you do it once a week instead? You must find the balance between the efficiency of your system and the adequacy of your effort.

Apply these ground rules as you institute the systems you will build throughout this book. If money is a touchy subject in your relationship, perhaps all you need is some organization and a reliable system that works for both of you. Remember, if this isn't enough to bring you into agreement, seek advice from a relationship expert.

> **note** You must find the balance between the efficiency of your system and the adequacy of your effort.

Summary

Congratulations! You've accomplished a lot in this chapter. Now you have systems for collecting all your transaction information and recording the data. You've learned some handy tricks for working around problem situations, and you're ready to move on to making your records agree with the bank's and exploring some computer-based options for maintaining your individual account registers. Later, in Chapter 8, "Learn More from Your Organized Data," we'll talk about ways to analyze your neatly captured numbers (those totals we created in your spreadsheet, for one thing). But first, let's move on to Chapter 2, "Getting the Figures to Match," and delve into balancing your accounts, a task that you'll find much easier with the progress you've made so far.

Getting the Figures to Match

2

*M*oney anxiety. Isn't that phrase redundant? It often seems like money is the main generator of anxiety in people's lives: If you have money, you worry about losing it, and if you don't have it, you worry about losing everything else.

For people who suffer from money anxiety, the pain is often sharpest when it's time to balance the checkbook. It's report-card time for adults: How well did you keep track of your spending? Did you record every transaction? Did you make any calculation errors? When you balance the account, will you find some mistake that caused checks to bounce or left you with less money than you thought you had?

What will it be this month: Pass or fail?

With pressure like that, it's no wonder that many people put off balancing their accounts. They let the statements pile up, add money to the account whenever they can, call the bank or go online to check their available balance, and try to rely on memory to guess whether the money in the account will be enough to cover whatever checks and debits haven't yet come in. Now that's anxiety!

If your reaction to a bank statement in the mail is to toss it aside and think, "Ugh! I don't want to know," there are things you can do to counteract your money anxiety—not eliminate it, but reduce it enough that you'll be able to sit down with each statement and balance your account before things really get out of control.

In this chapter:

* Learn how to balance your accounts by hand

* Explore the features available in financial software that would be most useful to you

* Explore options for using your computer to reconcile accounts semi- or fully automatically

* Discover how to troubleshoot when an account doesn't balance

* Learn how to back up financial data on your computer

Two things will make the process more pleasant:

- A user-friendly system
- Familiarity with that system

When you have a system for performing a task, you don't have to put a lot of thought into the task each time: You simply start with step 1. When that system is familiar to you from frequent use, you don't even have to look up what step 1 is; you know because you do it often.

In this chapter, you put together a system for balancing your accounts, either on paper or using your computer. When you choose from the various options presented here, always select the option that will make your system function well for you and that will encourage you to use it often.

Okay, deep breath: You're going to get these accounts balanced, so you'll never again fear the monthly arrival of the bank statement!

To do list

- ☐ Review the process for balancing your accounts on paper.
- ☐ Gather the necessary records, equipment, and materials.
- ☐ Balance your accounts.
- ☐ Troubleshoot to resolve any discrepancies.

Learning to Reconcile Your Accounts the Old-Fashioned Way

Okay, I admit it: There is really no need to balance your checking account by hand. With all of the software and online options available, the ability to maintain your balance with pencil, paper, and calculator is no longer required.

Nonetheless, knowing how to balance your account the old-fashioned way has its advantages. Even if you never plan to do the math yourself, it is valuable to understand what's happening as the software chugs away, so you can more easily resolve problems when they occur.

And they will occur. It happens to everybody sooner or later.

Most bank statements include a worksheet for balancing your account by hand. Give it a try next time you receive your statement, or work through the following exercise. At the very least, check out the "Troubleshooting to Find Discrepancies" section for tips on resolving the problem when your account won't balance. These tips will help even if you're a diehard computer reconciler.

If you've never reconciled your checking account, or if you used to but it's been a while, now is the perfect time to start fresh. Find your most recent account statement and use its opening balance and the transactions listed on it to begin your new reconciliation system.

A FIFTY-CENT WORD: RECONCILIATION

Reconciliation is the official term for balancing an account. When you reconcile successfully, all of your transactions are accounted for and your balance matches the institution's balance for that account.

You should reconcile your accounts as often as you need to in order to keep a handle on your balance and spending. Some people take comfort in reconciling every day or every time they make a deposit, but most are satisfied to do it once a month when the account statement arrives in the mail.

You'll need list

- ☐ Your most recent bank statement
- ☐ Registers for your checking account(s) and receipts or notes on unrecorded transactions
- ☐ Paper and pencil
- ☐ A calculator

The Basic Idea

To get a mental grip on how reconciliation works, remember that a checking account is a type of short-term loan. When you spend money from the account or deposit money into it, there is generally a delay of at least a couple of days between the time of the transaction and the time it is processed by the bank.

This is why you can't count on the bank's rendering of your account balance to be accurate. The balance printed on your ATM slips, shown in your account record on the bank's Web site, or given to you by the automated phone system or even a live teller is based only on transactions that have cleared the bank: The bank has no knowledge of checks you've written that the recipient has not yet cashed.

So, the best the bank can do is to tell you your cleared balance—useful information, but not enough to know whether you can take out $20 at the ATM without causing a check to bounce. Only you have all of the information to calculate your actual, up-to-the-minute balance.

To get ready to balance your account by hand, gather the equipment, records, and supplies in the You'll Need list that accompanies this section of the chapter, and prepare to reconcile.

The Basic Steps

With your materials ready, follow these steps to reconcile your bank account:

1. Check your deposits. Do all of the deposits on the statement appear in your check register? Note: Some banks list electronic deposits (for example, returns of purchases made with a debit card) not in the usual deposits section, but instead with electronic debits. If the statement shows that you have earned interest on this account, record the interest in your register.

2. Check your withdrawals. Does every withdrawal and expenditure on the statement appear in your register? You might have to check several sections of the statement for these: Checks, ATM transactions, and electronic debits, for example. If there is an account maintenance fee or you find additional ATM fees on the statement, record them in your register now.

After you have confirmed that all of the transactions on the statement appear in your register, follow these steps to calculate your account balance:

1. Record the ending balance shown on your account statement.

2. Subtract from that figure the total of all *expenditures* recorded in your register but not listed on your statement.

3. Add to the result of step 2 the total of all *deposits* recorded in your register but not listed on the statement.

The final figure should match the balance shown in your check register, as shown in this table.

Reconciling Your Account Balance

Step 1:	Ending balance shown on account statement:	$ _____
Step 2:	Total of all expenditures recorded in register but not listed on statement:	– $ _____
Step 3:	Total of all deposits recorded in register but not listed on statement:	+ $ _____
	Your current balance:	$ _____

Step 1 – Step 2 + Step 3 = your current balance. This figure should match the balance shown in your check register.

Troubleshooting to Find Discrepancies

Uh oh, it doesn't balance. You've double-checked your math, but something is still wrong. Now what?

First, compare the balance you've calculated to the balance the bank statement shows. Which is bigger? If your balance is greater than the bank's, you're probably missing an expenditure. If your balance is less, you might be missing a deposit.

Now look at the amount by which you're off. Sometimes that amount will ring a bell. Perhaps an overage of $7.50 will prompt you to confirm you've figured in the monthly account maintenance fee, or maybe something around $20 is likely to be one of those Amazon.com impulse purchases you sometimes forget to record. A deficit of $15.89 might remind you that you returned a defective CD a few weeks ago and they put the refund on your checking account Visa.

If pondering the amount doesn't bring a revelation, break the problem down into sections. Most bank statements provide subtotals that come in handy in this situation. Chances are you will find the discrepancy in one of these subsections. If your calculated balance is less than the bank's, add up your deposits and compare the total to the deposits subtotal on the statement. If your balance is higher than the bank's, try adding up all of your checks or all of your ATM transactions and comparing it to the subtotals shown on the statement.

If it still doesn't work, check all of your amounts again, figure by figure. Perhaps you've transposed numbers in one check amount, or perhaps you jotted down the wrong amount on an ATM deposit envelope.

> **tip**
>
> If your check register is a mess—items crossed out or squeezed in between lines, with the running balance rewritten several times—draw a big, bold line under the last item written in the register and start over. On the first blank line, write, "Reconciled balance as of [date]," and record the amount you just calculated. Now you can resume recording new transactions and keep an accurate running balance.

Organized AtoZ Enough

Rarely, you'll find an actual error in the bank statement. If it's a large enough amount, call the bank and ask them to correct the error; if it's not worth the trouble, adjust your records and get on with your day. Remember the value of your time: Is a $1 refund worth 15 minutes on the phone? If not, record a $1 debit in your register for Bank Error to correct your balance.

REPLACING LOST PAPERS

Suppose you're ready to turn over a new leaf and finally get your bank accounts balanced but you can't find some of your recent statements. Argh! What now?

Don't fret: Most documents can be retrieved from their sources. You can begin your new system with just your most recent bank statement, but if you really want to start with January, contact your bank. It should be able to provide you with duplicates of your statements, probably for a fee; it might also be able to give you access to the data online as an alternative to paper copies. Either way, the data exists somewhere within the bank's system; it's not lost forever.

The same is true of just about any record or statement you receive from another company. If you need past utility or phone bills, contact each utility for its procedure. The person who handles payroll for your employer can tell you how to obtain old check stubs or an earnings summary for the year. Your broker should be able to help you track down past investment statements. You can even obtain copies of past tax returns from the IRS. Use Form 4506 to get an exact copy for a fee or Form 4506-T for a free transcript, which is acceptable for most purposes. Visit www.IRS.gov and download the forms or call 800-829-1040 to request the forms by mail.

To do list

- ❏ Explore the various software options available.
- ❏ Learn how to use the assisted reconciliation function.
- ❏ Take advantage of the ability to categorize transactions.
- ❏ Review other advanced functions included with some programs.
- ❏ Choose and set up financial software.

Letting Your Computer Do the Work

Remember that happy moment back in school when you were finally allowed to use a calculator? Until then, you had to show your work, performing all of your calculations with paper and pencil. Eventually, after years of doing it all by hand, you earned the privilege of punching it all into a calculator and letting the machine do the grunt work.

That day has arrived once again. Now that you know how to balance your checkbook by hand, you've earned the right to let your computer do it for you. (If you've skipped the previous section, let me again encourage you to at least familiarize yourself with the process. It really does help when problems crop up with electronic balancing.)

You'll need list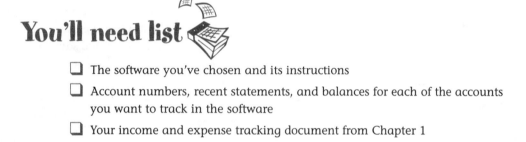

- [ ] The software you've chosen and its instructions
- [ ] Account numbers, recent statements, and balances for each of the accounts you want to track in the software
- [ ] Your income and expense tracking document from Chapter 1

Financial Software Options

If you want to computerize your finances, you have a lot of software choices—so many that you might find it difficult to determine the best one for you. The choice is further complicated by the ongoing revisions and improvements software manufacturers make to their products, meaning that whatever you buy today will probably be reincarnated by next year.

Because so many software options are available, it's beyond the scope of this book to explore each of them in detail. Instead, let's consider the basic components that make up most of these products and then determine which of those components you need so you can make a more educated buying decision.

Assisted Reconciliation

This is one of the best features of any financial management software. The program walks you through the reconciliation of your accounts, prompting you to fill in certain information (the closing balance from your statement, any interest or fees, and so on); then it allows you to check off cleared transactions and performs all of the calculations for you. The reconciliation process is much quicker and more accurate this way, and this feature alone makes the software worth the price for many people.

Categorized Transactions

Along with assisted reconciliation, the ability to label your transactions with categories such as Utilities, Entertainment, and Medical Expenses makes financial software invaluable for budgeting and tracking your income and spending. With most programs, you can sort your expenditures by category and see at a glance how much of your income is going to any of your categories. You can also use subcategories—for example, putting Water, Gas, and Electric all under Utilities— so you can then see totals for each of the utilities as well as a total for the group.

You can even split a single transaction across multiple categories (see Figure 2.1). For example, if you spend $22 at the gas station but only $20 was for gas, you can record the purchase as a single transaction and categorize $20 of it as Gas and the other $2 as Snacks or Lottery Tickets, all in one step. You can even separate the sales tax on a purchase if you want to track it separately. Categorizing saves innumerable hours of on-paper analysis and allows you to see the big picture of your bills and spending habits.

FIGURE 2.1

Most finance-management software allows you to split a transaction into more than one category, as in this example from QuickBooks.

Other Functions

Most finance-management software offers a range of other options and features, including

- **Reports and budgeting**—Most programs offer the ability to create a budget and generate reports to see your data in a variety of ways. It might take some effort to figure out how to create a report that tells you exactly what you want to know in the exact way you want to see it, but in many cases it's easier and more accurate than doing it manually.

- **Recurring transactions**—Most programs allow you to set up recurring transactions, so you don't have to enter each instance of a payment that is taken out automatically each month. You can also set reminders for yourself to pay items on a certain date or frequency.

- **Online services**—Some programs can be used in conjunction with online services offered by your bank, such as online bill-paying, automatic bill-paying, and downloading of account statements directly into your financial software. The most advanced software products can make managing your accounts almost completely automated (not necessarily desirable if your goal is to be more familiar with the details of your finances).

- **Investment functions**—The advanced versions of software such as Quicken and Microsoft Money offer the ability to track your investments, improve your investing skills and knowledge, and generate tax reports.

- **Business-related functions**—Certain products, such as Quicken Premier Home & Business, any of the QuickBooks products, and Microsoft Money Small Business, are geared toward small business owners. These products can also be used to manage your personal finances, but if you are not a business owner, they're probably more than you need.

Choosing and Setting Up Your Software Product

Time to hit the Net! Keeping the previously mentioned components in mind, check out the Web sites of the software manufacturers that interest you. Those mentioned here are Quicken and QuickBooks, produced by Intuit (www.intuit.com), and Microsoft Money (www.microsoft.com/money/default.asp). Also check out Figures 2.2 and 2.3 for comparison charts from each of these Web sites. Other products might be available that could work for you as well, so look around until you find the one that most appeals to you.

Another popular bookkeeping software you might encounter in your research is Peachtree Accounting (www.peachtree.com). This product is excellent for businesses and people with an accounting background, but I strongly advise against it for residential users and sole proprietors who are not extremely well-versed in accounting practices. It is far more software than most users need for tracking their personal finances and, in my experience, people who have not studied accounting find it very confusing.

note Don't buy more software than you need. If your goal is to get your personal checking account under control, don't buy an accounting software for businesses and confuse yourself with the many options it offers that you don't need.

Organized A to Z Enough

Setup procedures differ from one software to the next, and often the process has many steps designed to customize the program to your needs. As you dive in to setting up your new program, here are some universal tips:

Which Quicken 2004 for Windows product is right for you?	Deluxe	Premier	Premier Home & Business
Manage Your Personal Finances			
Easy step-by-step setup	✓	✓	✓
Balance your checkbook	✓	✓	✓
Reports & graphs show where your money goes	✓	✓	✓
Pay bills - write or print checks, or pay online*	✓	✓	✓
Create & manage budgets, forecast cash flow	✓	✓	✓
Download bank & credit card transactions*	✓	✓	✓
Track tax data and transfer to TurboTax®*	✓	✓	✓
Find ways to reduce debt	✓	✓	✓
Monitor your total net worth	✓	✓	✓
Download & track investments, 401(k) & IRA*	✓	✓	✓
Monitor your asset allocation	✓	✓	✓
Plan for retirement, college or a new home	✓	✓	✓
Find hidden tax deductions	✓	✓	✓
Optimize Your Investments & Taxes			
Analyze your portfolio		✓	✓
See a consolidated report of investing activity		✓	✓
Compare investments to market indexes*		✓	✓
Get investing insights to help improve performance*		✓	✓
Compare the Morningstar Rating™ on your funds*		✓	✓
Generate Schedule A, B & D tax reports		✓	✓
Learn from step-by step investment tutorials		✓	✓
Find ways to minimize capital gains taxes		✓	✓
Get the Business Features You Need			
Create customizable estimates & invoices			✓
Generate business reports & graphs			✓
Automatically track Schedule C items			✓
Track vehicle mileage for tax purposes			✓
Track multiple jobs per customer			✓
Monitor unpaid invoices (receivables)			✓
Track accounts payable & reimbursables			✓
Synchronize with Palm, ACT! & Outlook†			✓
Create a mini-business plan			✓
Get guidance for starting & running a business			✓

- **Read the materials that come with the software before you begin—** The box often has the best summary of a product's features. Decide which of these you will use and which you will not; most programs allow you to turn on only portions of the program and leave unneeded functions inactive but available to add later.

- **Decide who will be using the software**—Will you need more than one user identity?

- **Have your account numbers ready to plug in during the setup procedure**—To begin, it's easiest to enter just your checking account; you can add other accounts such as credit cards later if you want.

FIGURE 2.3

This comparison chart from www.microsoft.com/money/default.asp shows the features available in various Microsoft Money products.

- **Have your categories figured out**—Every software uses an expense category list (the technical term is *chart of accounts*) to allow you to note what you're spending your money on and then generate reports to analyze your spending. Begin with the categories you identified in Chapter 1, "Tracking Your Money."

- **Make sure you have the basics down before you venture into the fancy stuff**—Keep your goal in mind and meet it before you move on to something else. For example, if your goal is to use money-management software to give you an error-free, balanced personal checking account with no overdrafts, make sure you achieve that goal before you delve into the other functions that might be included with your software, such as online banking, investing, or creating a budget. (In Chapter 8, "Learn More from Your Organized Data," I give you some first steps in using your newly organized data to advance to more complicated projects.)

AIRLINE MILES AND OTHER NOT-EXACTLY-MONEY ASSETS

Would you like to track things like airline miles or contributions to a child's Upromise college fund (www.upromise.org) within the same system you use for your checking account? You can! Simply set up an account for each within your software. (I classify mine as cash accounts and exclude them from reports showing my "real-money" assets.) Whenever you add money to your Upromise account or gain or use airline miles, enter the information as you would a cash transaction.

To do list

- ☐ Choose a method to use for backing up your files.
- ☐ Determine which files you will back up on a regular basis.
- ☐ Select safe storage for your backup disks.

Backing Up Financial Data on Your Computer

Exercise. Flossing. Cleaning the gutters. Backing up computer files. All things we know we should do, but often don't.

I can't help you with the first three. (Actually, I could motivate you with gum-disease horror stories courtesy of my friend the dental hygienist, but I won't.) However, backing up computer files becomes especially important when you're tracking your entire financial life electronically, so let's give it a shot.

Why don't we do it?

- We don't know how.
- The files are too big for floppy disks.
- We don't know which file(s) to save.
- We don't have the necessary equipment or software.
- We keep forgetting.

You'll need list

- ☐ Disks or rewriteable CDs
- ☐ Software to perform the backup function (either included with your computer system or purchased separately)

Choosing a Backup Method

This is one of those tasks that sounds simple, but when you get into it, it can become maddeningly complex. In the process of writing this book, I discovered that the backup utility in Windows XP works with disks only, not CDs. I had about 900 MB of data to back up, and a floppy disk holds just over 1 MB, so that wasn't going to work. (See the sidebar "How Big Is MB?")

I tinkered and got frustrated and finally tried something so obvious I was sure it wouldn't work. I simply dragged and dropped a file from the C: drive to the E: drive, where my blank CD was waiting expectantly. Lo and behold, it worked. So, now I know that to back up my files, I copy the pertinent folders to E:, then open E:, and click Write These Files to CD. (And yes, I will do regular backups now, I promise.)

If the same thing works for you, I'll be elated and also surprised. Every computer is different, whether due to the variety of operating systems available or quirks introduced when you (or your computer consultant) set it up. But creating a backup routine is important and worth pursuing—annoying as it is—so keep trying until you find a way.

When you've determined how to back up your files and which files to back up, write down the steps so you won't have to figure it out again if you forget to back up for a few months. Then add this task to your calendar, planner, or to-do list to remind yourself to perform regular backups.

Deciding Which Files to Back Up

At the very least, back up your financial management software from within the program by following its instructions, and make a disk copy of any other documents you use to manage your finances. For example, I use the backup function built in to QuickBooks to create backup copies of my QuickBooks files on floppy disks (see Figure 2.4), and I copy the subdirectories containing my most critical business and personal files onto CDs. It helps that my computer files are organized so I can quickly determine what to copy and what to skip, but that's a whole other book.

FIGURE 2.4

QuickBooks (shown here) and other finance-management software provide a backup function built in to the program that allows you to save to your hard drive or to disk.

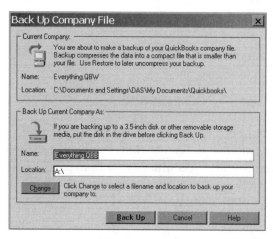

As you can see from the data in "How Big Is MB?" simply copying your entire hard drive is not realistic. You need to do at least some file selection. But if you use Windows and you save all of the files you create to the My Documents folder or to subfolders within My Documents, you can simply back up the entire My Documents folder to a CD. That's pretty darn convenient.

HOW BIG IS MB?

Here are some handy figures for calculating how much storage space your backup files will require.

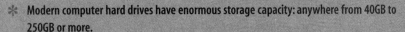

* *GB* means *gigabyte* and is the largest measurement used in basic computer conversations; a *byte* is the smallest increment.

   1GB = 1,024 megabytes (MB) = 1 billion bytes

   1MB = 1,024 kilobytes (KB)

   1KB = 1,024 bytes

* Modern computer hard drives have enormous storage capacity: anywhere from 40GB to 250GB or more.

* A typical CD-R holds 650MB, which is plenty of room for a lot of data files and photos, but nowhere near enough for your entire hard drive. It takes two CD-Rs to back up my important data folders, which, at a total of about 900MB, are a small subset of the 7GB currently in use on my computer.

* A typical 3.5" floppy disk holds 1.44 MB. That's good for quite a few Word files, but probably not enough for an entire subdirectory and of limited use for digital photos. I use one disk to back up my QuickBooks files.

* Word processing documents tend to be relatively small. Each chapter of this book is only about 100 KB, so the whole thing (without illustrations) would fit on one floppy disk. Digital photos and audio and video files, however, tend to be huge: A single .bmp photo file might be between 2 MB and 8 MB, or more than twice the size of all the text in this book.

Storing Your Backup Disks

If you're backing up your computer files only in case your computer crashes, you can simply keep the disks in a drawer. If you want to protect them in case of fire or theft as well, you need to take an extra step or two. You can either store your disks offsite or store them in your home with added protection.

If you choose offsite storage and you're using rewriteable disks, you might find it easiest to have two sets of disks: Create one set and put it in storage; next time, back up to a second set of disks, take them to your storage place, and swap the second set for the first. The third time you do your backup, use the first set of disks and retrieve the second set to reuse the next time. Here are some potential offsite storage solutions:

- **Trade with a friend or neighbor**—Choose someone whom you trust not to snoop in your files, of course. Or if you trust no one that fully, password-protect the disks. Then take a set of backup disks with you each time you see that person, or set a regular date to trade. You don't have to take special measures to protect each other's disks—just store them as you would any of your other computer media. The advantage of this option is that it's highly unlikely both your home and your friend's will be burglarized or destroyed in a disaster at the exact same time. If something happens to your computer, you'll have the files at your friend's place, and if something happens to them there, you still have your original data at home. This option has the added bonus of a built-in reminder: Every time you see this person, you'll remember to back up your files.

- **At work**—Store your disks in a locked drawer in your desk or locker at work. This way, they're safe if something happens at home and you can access them as often as you go to work.

- **Safe deposit box**—If you already use a safe deposit box, you could add your disks to it and get more value for your monthly rental fee. You can be sure they're safe in this environment, although your access is somewhat limited.

- **Fire safe**—If you want to store your disks at home, you might think the fire safe you already have is all you need. You might be right, but double-check its ability to protect computer media. According to fire safe manufacturer Sentry (www.sentrysafe.com), paper products can withstand heat up to 450° F, but computer disks, audio and video cassettes, photo negatives, and other delicate items can be damaged at just 125° F. Sentry makes a few safes that are intended to protect computer media (see Figure 2.5).

Using a Disk-Free Option: Online Storage

If you don't want to mess with disks and don't mind paying a monthly fee, check out the many companies offering online storage for your backup files. The basic idea is that you send your files to the company's computer (which is much larger and more sophisticated than yours) via the Internet and it stores them for you in a much safer environment than your own. Online storage has several advantages, including unlimited storage capacity (but the more space you rent, the more you pay) and none of the damage risks associated with disks and CDs. It also provides a solution for those who do not have the equipment or software to back up to CD, and it also allows you to access your files from any computer with Internet access, so it's convenient for frequent travelers.

FIGURE 2.5

Every household should have a fire safe! Its contents could be all you have left to rebuild your life after a fire or natural disaster. Visit www. sentrysafe.com for product information and testimonials.

One such company, IBackup (www.ibackup.com; see Figure 2.6), promises vigorous protection from earthquakes, fires, break-ins (onsite as well as hackers), and server crashes and offers a variety of storage space rental options, from 50MB for just $3 per month up to 100GB for $800 per month. Its 4GB for $14.95 per month should be adequate for most households.

FIGURE 2.6

IBackup (www. ibackup.com) offers online storage of your electronic files.

Summary

Doesn't that feel better? You'll sleep well tonight: You have a great system for keeping your accounts reconciled, so your days of wondering whether there's money in the checking account are over! That is, if you use your new system....

Remember, an organizing tool's effectiveness is dependent on your consistent and complete use of it. In the next chapter, we look at ways to change your habits so your new financial-management system will work to its full potential for you.

In this chapter, you've learned how to reconcile your accounts the old-fashioned way (with pencil and paper) and you've reviewed a number of finance-management software options. You've also learned to troubleshoot discrepancies that occur during your reconciliation and some important techniques for backing up your financial information. In Chapter 3, "Avoiding Late Fees and Overdrafts," you'll establish a proactive approach to bill-paying and put safeguards in place to prevent late fees and overdrafts.

Avoiding Late Fees
and Overdrafts

3

In this chapter:

* Finding a system that works for you

* Choosing the best payment method

* Minimizing bill-paying hassles

* Learning to stick with your system

Just when you think you've finally got it together, BAM!, in comes another overdraft notice. It's enough to make you throw up your hands in defeat.

Don't despair. With all you've accomplished in the first two chapters, you're well on your way to perfecting every aspect of your financial organization. You have a system for tracking your income and expenses and for keeping your accounts balanced; add the skills and tricks you learn in this chapter and you just might make bounced checks and overdrafts a thing of the past.

In this chapter, you add to your financial organization with a reliable bill-paying system. We also consider some of the intangibles professional organizers look for when a client cries, "Why can't I just make myself do this?!?" With sharper techniques and clearer motivation, you'll be on your way to a life free of late fees and those dreaded overdraft notices.

Ready? Let's get those bills handled!

To do list

☐ Discover the factors that impact your ability to manage your finances.

☐ Find out whether your work style is "sprinter" or "jogger."

☐ Incorporate what has worked in the past into your new system.

☐ Learn how to share a joint account without constant overdrafts.

When Time Flies, So Does Money: Finding a System for On-Time Payments

You've heard the expression, "Time is money," perhaps from a boss who doesn't believe in lunch breaks. Indeed, this saying is typically used to motivate others, not oneself, but it's worth internalizing. It becomes much more palatable when you're using it for your own benefit, not that of a company that gives you too little of both time and money to begin with!

Professional organizers know that time is an exhaustible resource, just like money, and it's even more precious because, unlike money, there is an absolute limit to the amount of time you can "make" in a day. We also know that mismanaging one invariably costs you more of the other: If you neglect money matters, you'll have to spend time to get back on track, and if you're not careful with your time, you'll end up losing money somewhere, somehow.

And so it goes with your personal finances. If you don't have a system for paying bills on time, you'll incur late charges and possibly damage your credit rating. If you don't keep your financial records up-to-date with regularly scheduled reconciliation times, you'll bounce checks and incur still more fees and ill will from creditors.

I believe that awareness is half the battle in all organizing challenges; therefore, if you struggle with time management as it relates to your finances, you'll make huge strides toward helping yourself to improve if you become aware of a few things:

- What makes on-time payment difficult for you?
- How do you approach the task of bill-paying?
- What methods have worked best for you in the past?
- What can you do to get yourself on-track with bill-paying?
- What special money-management issues do you face, including managing shared accounts?

The following sections help you explore all of these questions in more detail, so you're better able to come up with a bill-paying system that works for you.

What Makes This So Hard for You?

Is it solely a time-management issue in that you just forget to do it? Or is there an emotional component? Often we procrastinate or avoid a task without even realizing we're doing it, and the reason is an emotional one. It could be fear: Dealing with bill-paying stirs up your insecurity and anxiety about money, success, and making something of yourself. It could be resentment: You resent having to pay money for some things, whether it's substandard phone service or a loan you had to take to pay for something that turned out to be a rip-off.

It could be that old bugaboo, perfectionism: If you can't do it perfectly, completely, on time, every time, then your heart's just not in doing it at all. It could be boredom: This is a pretty boring task, and many people have a low tolerance for duties that do not engage the imagination. It could be confusion: You just don't "get" money or your current system is too complex.

Acknowledge the factors that are keeping you from fully engaging yourself in this project. Accept that these are valid emotions, and stop judging yourself for having them.

Are You a Sprinter or a Jogger?

I learned this one from Wilma Fellman, author of *Finding a Career That Works for You*. If you're a *jogger*, you prefer to do a little at a time, taking a steady pace and completing projects in a more or less peaceful, predictable manner. If you're a *sprinter*, you tend to complete projects in bursts of energy, focusing your entire being on one thing for a short period of time and then walking away from it to regroup for a while. A jogger prefers to enter transactions into a financial management system every day; a sprinter prefers to do them in a batch once every week or so.

Sprinters are much more susceptible to spontaneity, and at times much more productive because of it. The inherent problem with a spontaneous approach to money management is that the consequences of falling behind and catching back up tend to be more severe than in other areas of life.

If you're a sprinter, endeavor to create just enough structure to prevent missed deadlines while still allowing for your naturally spontaneous nature.

What Has Worked in the Past?

If there was a time when you were on top of the bills, what was different? Was there someone in your life who served as an anchor or motivator to keep you on track? Did you have more money, or less? Were there fewer bills? Assess what has worked for you and look for ways to bring it back into your current system.

What Do You Do Now to Finally Get It Done?

Do you pull an all-nighter before tax day? Do you rely on overdraft protection to cover you and then use your panic to motivate you into getting the bills settled for another couple weeks? Perhaps you thrive on adrenaline—the rush of saving the day at the last possible minute. Do you find it harder to motivate yourself to pay bills when you have a smaller amount of funds available? It could be that working in fine detail to allocate each dollar precisely is just too overwhelming for you. Does it take someone else prodding you into action (the angry spouse, the tsk-tsking mother, the relentless bill collector)? Maybe that's because you really don't want to have to do it anyway.

What parts of all of that can you incorporate into a more effective system? Think carefully about this. The answer might be that you should delegate this task to someone else; if that's not realistic, it will be all the more important for you to find a system that gives you maximum accuracy for minimum effort.

After you've made these observations, it's time to boil it all down into one big reality check: What level of organization is realistic for you? Again, set aside self-criticism and judgment, be objective, and be honest. Is it likely that you (and those holding joint accounts with you) are going to be able to maintain perfect accuracy, or do you need a system that allows a margin of error?

Now is not the time for ambition! Let's have none of the "I should" and "I'll try harder" and "I'll do better". This is about finding a system that works for you, not contorting yourself to work for the system.

Doing Damage Control with "Safety Valve" Accounts

Consider how one couple's acceptance of reality led to a brilliant idea for creating a workable system for paying bills on time. Like every other couple, Beth and her husband hate bouncing checks, but when two people use a single checking account, it's easy to lose track of the available balance and spend yourselves into overdraft. This problem can occur for a number of reasons:

- One of you is a spender and the other a saver.
- One is good at tracking spending and the other is not.

- The one who pays the household bills doesn't always communicate the balance to the other.
- One or both rely on the ATM's balance statement instead of their own calculations.

When you're sharing something tangible, like cereal or shampoo, it's easy to tell when it's all gone. Not so with money. People using the old cash-under-the-mattress system never had our problems: The money was either there or it wasn't—no line of credit, no check-clearing period. Nowadays, the money we spend exists mostly as data in a computer, and transactions rarely require cash in hand. This makes it easy for both of you to spend the same dollar—sometimes more than once!

Beth accepted that there was no way she and her husband could expect to never bounce another check—they're just not able to be that precise. What she could do, though, was minimize the damage. She made a few changes and immediately saw a huge improvement.

Follow Beth's system to address this problem for yourself:

1. Open two new checking accounts: one for you and one for your spouse. These can be individual or joint accounts, but each must be used by only one of you. You will now have the old joint checking account (the main account) and two new ones (we'll call these the safety valves).

2. Do not carry checks or ATM cards for the main account in your purse or wallet. File them away at home.

3. Deposit all income from both of you into the main account.

4. Pay the big household bills (mortgage, insurance, utilities) from the main account.

5. Transfer a set amount from the main account into each of the safety-valve accounts, making absolutely sure you've left enough in the main account to cover the checks you sent out for bills.

6. Use your safety valve for your day-to-day purchases and cash withdrawals at the ATM. *Never* transfer money from the main account into a safety valve without thoroughly balancing the main account!

7. The person who pays the bills from the main account keeps that account balanced and reconciles the bank statement. Each of you is responsible for balancing your own safety valve account.

This system eases a lot of tension in couples where one or both aren't that great at managing money. As Beth notes, they still bounce checks from the safety valve accounts once in a while, but at least they know that the most important bills are always paid, and they no longer argue over whose fault it is that the account was overdrawn. This way, they can still have a joint account, something they believe in as a symbol of marital cooperation, but they can also minimize the impact of their slip-ups on each other's nerves and on their overall credit rating.

Finding the Best Way to Pay

The companies you owe money to are very helpful when it's time to pay them; most provide a number of ways to give them money, whether by mail, phone, their Web site, your bank's Web site, or in person, and most will take various forms of money as well: paper check, one-time or recurring automatic transfer from checking, credit card, money order, cash, chickens. (Chickens are the least common.)

With such a dazzling array of fabulous ways to separate yourself from your funds, how can you choose which is best? Consider these questions:

- **How comfortable are you with technology?**—Are you able to retain control when weird things start happening with your computer, or would you panic if your screen went blank just after you entered your credit card number and just before you clicked Submit? Would it be better for your blood pressure to stick with paper checks and the good ol' postal service?

- **How important is saving time to you?**—Are you willing to endure some new processes and additional expenses if they will save you time? In your experience, has the so-called time savings of a computerized system actually taken longer than doing the task the old-fashioned way?

- **How reliable is your Internet connection?**—If you get the unexpected "Goodbye" from AOL on a regular basis, think twice before you delve into online banking and bill-paying.

- **Do the particular workings of your mind require that you choose one payment method and use it for all of your bills?**—Or are you okay with using different methods for different payees, depending on the circumstances of each?

This should give you some idea of which of the payment options in the next section will be best for you.

SHARE WITH A FRIEND

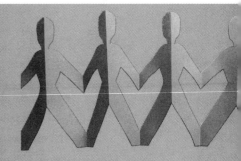

If you find that you can easily tell a friend how to set up a money management system but you sometimes struggle to handle your own, do what professional organizers do: Trade! Don't tell them I told you, but organizers sometimes need an organizer. We, too, become emotionally paralyzed with our own papers and clutter, even as we remain efficient and upbeat when helping a client.

Find a friend who also has a hard time with the process and partner up. Tell each other the amount of money available, trade checkbooks, and write out each other's bills. It works because the task is not nearly as emotional when you're dealing with someone else's money (or belongings or paperwork). If you like it, tackle each other's closets!

To do list

- ☐ Set up a bill-paying system based on paper, software, or the Internet.
- ☐ Use your system.

Less Painful Bill-Paying

Next I'm going to give you three examples of bill-paying systems. Keep in mind that you can mix and match components from each if you choose, but to be effective, whatever system you end up with should have

- A foolproof method for getting the bills into the system. (This is covered in detail in the next chapter.)
- A cue for when to pay the bill.
- Up-to-date financial data to tell you whether you have the money to pay the bill.
- Supplies for paying the bill and sending the payment.
- An easy way to check whether and with which method you paid the bill. (I call this a "Did I Pay That?" document.)

Keeping those points in mind, begin with one of the following three options and customize at will.

You'll need list

❑ Your bills and bill-paying supplies: checkbook or bank card, stamps, blank envelopes, and return address labels

❑ Your computer and Internet connection

❑ The income and expense tracking document you created in Chapter 1

❑ Personal finance software such as Quicken or Microsoft Money (optional)

Option 1: An All-Paper System

If you skipped the "Letting Your Computer Do the Work" section in Chapter 2, "Getting the Figures to Match," this is the option for you. Here are the steps you'll follow if you choose to pay and record bill payments by hand:

1. Receive paper bills via regular mail.

2. Open each bill and discard the outer envelope. On the return envelope, write the amount and date due in pencil where the stamp will go. Stuff the bill into the return envelope and add it to the others waiting to be paid.

3. If you don't already have a schedule for paying bills, create one: Consider when you will have money (your pay dates), when you have to give money away (the due dates on the bills), and your temperament (sprinter or jogger) to determine how often you must tend to this task; then write it into your calendar.

4. On bill-paying day, gather your bills, checkbook and register, blank envelopes, return address labels, and stamps. You'll also need the income and expense tracking document you created in Chapter 1, "Tracking Your Money," or draw up a separate tracking sheet just for bill-paying (see Figure 3.1).

5. Write a check for each bill and enter it into your check register and your bill-paying tracking document.

6. File the statement portion of the bill if you keep them. (You'll learn more about filing systems in Chapter 5, "Here to Stay: Storing Documents for Easy Retrieval.")

7. Put the bill in the return envelope, stamp it, add your return address, and mail it. If you want to wait until closer to the due date to mail it, don't put the stamp on yet: Set the bills aside in a designated place, in order by the due date penciled in at the stamp spot, and each day choose the ones you're going to mail, stamp them, and send them out.

FIGURE 3.1

If you don't want to record bill-paying in your income and expense tracking document, create a separate "Did I Pay That?" record like the one shown here. You can use any lined paper or a common ledger book. Use one page per month, and write your regularly recurring bills in the same order each month. Add occasional or one-time bills after the regular ones each month as needed.

Did I Pay that? — June 04

Bill	Date Due	Amt. Due	Date Paid	Amt. Paid
Mortgage	6 - 1 - 04	$932.04	5 - 28 - 04	$932.04
Car insurance	6 - 15 - 04	$155.00	6 - 17 - 04	$155.00
Electric bill	6 - 8 - 04	$62.00	6 - 2 - 04	$62.00
Gas bill	6 - 21 - 04	$18.00		
Cable	6 - 25 - 04	$48.00		
Newspaper	6 - 30 - 04	$8.00	6 - 15 - 04	$10.00

Special Problem: Medical Bills

One of the most challenging aspects of paper management for my clients is keeping track of medical bills. Often we don't pay a medical bill right away because we're waiting to see what the insurance company is going to do about it or we're not able to pay the entire amount all at once.

This is when the March of the Duplicates begins. It reminds me of a child asking for something: "Can I have it now?...How 'bout now?...Okay, now?...What about now?" Anyone to whom you owe money is likely to remind you about it, but it seems that medical billers are the most frequent.

tip Bill-paying might be distasteful, but it doesn't have to actually taste bad. Instead of licking envelopes, use a glue stick to seal them. *Clever Client*

Chaos ensues when you already have a paper-management problem and you end up with multiple bills for the same service. You might pay part of one of them and even write a note to yourself on the bill and then find another copy of it the next day and wonder whether you imagined what you did the day before!

Don't wreck your health worrying about medical bills; use your new system to keep them organized. Here's the key to solving this problem before it begins:

1. Whenever you have a medical event, start a folder. Label it with the date, what happened, and where you went for treatment.

2. When documents begin marching into your mailbox regarding this event, escort them straight into the folder. Add a subfolder for each biller that contacts you, so you end up with, for example, a main folder called Broken Leg, 5-23-04, General Hosp. with subfolders labeled Hospital Bill, Lab Bill, X-rays, and Specialist.

3. When you receive a duplicate of a bill you already have, staple them together and file them in the correct subfolder. Don't just throw away the older bill and keep the newest copy—you might need to refer to that first one for the original bill date, and newer versions of the bill might contain updated insurance payment information. Sometimes the treatment codes and prices even change mysteriously; you'll want to know that. You might eventually end up with a thick packet of different iterations of the same bill; this is okay.

4. Add another subfolder labeled Explanation of Benefits for the statements you'll begin receiving from your insurance company. It would be nice if they would send one EOB per biller, per event, so you could just file each EOB in the appropriate biller's folder, but they usually don't.

5. Create a document similar to the one in Figure 3.2 to keep track of where you stand with each bill. You can make notes on this tracking document or on separate sheets. If you have to call about one of the bills, write your notes on any scrap paper during the call; when you hang up, add the date and the name of the person(s) you were talking to and file it in the subfolder for that bill.

6. When the event is finally resolved and paid for, file the entire folder. You should hold onto records like these for a few years, until you're very sure that everyone was paid and your insurance company isn't going to come back to you for more information.

If you think this seems like overkill, you must have great insurance!

tip
You can track any special billing situation with a template based on the one shown here for medical bills. This can be useful for any financial event with multiple steps, such as a home improvement or repair project.

FIGURE 3.2

Create a separate tracking document like this to keep on top of medical bills.

My insurance notes: $15 copay, $500 deductible

Event Date	Description	Pd at Site	Bill 1: Biller: Dr. Smith							Notes:
6/12/2004	Doctor visit-- headaches	$15	Date Rec'd	Date Due	Total	Minus Insurance Pd	Amt I Owe	Amt Pd	Date Pd	Haven't fulfilled deductible yet.
			6/24/2004	7/1/2004	$150	0	$135	$135	6/29/2004	
		$0	Bill 2: Biller: TechLabs							Notes:
			Date Rec'd	Date Due	Total	Minus Insurance Pd	Amt I Owe			
			6/26/2004	7/6/2004	$55	0	$55			Disputing this--waiting for info from ins. co.
			Bill 3: Biller:							Notes:
			Date Rec'd	Date Due	Total	Minus Insurance Pd	Amt I Owe			
			Bill 4: Biller:							Notes:
			Date Rec'd	Date Due	Total	Minus Insurance Pd	Amt I Owe			
			Bill 5: Biller:							Notes:
			Date Rec'd	Date Due	Total	Minus Insurance Pd	Amt I Owe			
			Bill 6: Biller:							Notes:
			Date Rec'd	Date Due	Total	Minus Insurance Pd	Amt I Owe			

Event Date	Description	Pd at Site	Bill 1: Biller:							Notes:
7/3/2004	Emergency room-- broken wrist	$0	Date Rec'd	Date Due	Total	Minus Insurance Pd	Amt I Owe	Amt Pd	Date Pd	
										Will be a bill for ER doc.
			Bill 2: Biller:							Notes:
			Date Rec'd	Date Due	Total	Minus Insurance Pd	Amt I Owe	Amt Pd	Date Pd	
										Might get a separate bill for x-ray.
			Bill 3: Biller:							Notes:
			Date Rec'd	Date Due	Total	Minus Insurance Pd	Amt I Owe	Amt Pd	Date Pd	
										Might get a separate bill for orthopedist.
			Bill 4: Biller:							Notes:
			Date Rec'd	Date Due	Total	Minus Insurance Pd	Amt I Owe	Amt Pd	Date Pd	
										Probably a separate bill for hospital.
			Bill 5: Biller:							Notes:
			Date Rec'd	Date Due	Total	Minus Insurance Pd	Amt I Owe	Amt Pd	Date Pd	
										Shouldn't be a lab bill.
			Bill 6: Biller:							Notes:
			Date Rec'd	Date Due	Total	Minus Insurance Pd	Amt I Owe	Amt Pd	Date Pd	

Option 2: A Software-Based System

If you chose a software product for managing your accounts in Chapter 2, this example will probably be the most appealing to you. Here are the steps you'll follow if you use personal finance software to manage bill payment:

1. Receive paper bills via regular mail or bill-ready notifications via email.

2. For paper bills, open each bill and discard the outer envelope. On the return envelope, write the amount and date due in pencil where the stamp will go; then stuff the bill into the return envelope. For e-bills, print the notice. Add the bills to others waiting to be paid.

3. If you don't already have a schedule for paying bills, create one: Consider when you will have money (your pay dates), when you have to give money away (the due dates on the bills), and your temperament (sprinter or jogger) to determine how often you must tend to this task. Then write it into your calendar. You can also set up reminders in your software, but don't rely solely on this method because the reminders will only work when you're in the software!

4. On bill-paying day, gather your bills, checkbook, bank card, blank envelopes, return address labels, and stamps, and sit down at the computer.

5. Prepare a payment for each bill, either by paper check or online using your bank card.

6. Open your money-management program and record each payment. Note the method you used to pay it (check, debit, and so on). If paying electronically, record your confirmation number in the transaction's memo field. Use the report features in your software to create your "Did I Pay That?" document as needed.

7. File the printout or statement portion of the bill if you keep them. (You'll learn more about filing systems in the next chapter.)

8. For each bill you're paying by mail, put the bill in the return envelope, stamp it, add your return address, and mail it. If you want to wait until closer to the due date to mail it, don't put the stamp on it yet: Set the bills aside in a designated spot, in order by the due date penciled in at the stamp spot; then, each day choose the ones you're going to mail, stamp them, and send them out.

caution If you're really techno-savvy, you might have noticed that the latest versions of money-management software such as Quicken and Microsoft Money are capable of communicating directly with your bank via your online banking feature. This means your software can download your transactions and even reconcile itself using information from your bank, with little or no involvement on your part. I strongly recommend that you do *not* do this if your goal is to be more aware of what's happening with your finances: It might be less work for you, but it might also distance you too far from the details.

Option 3: A Web-Based System

If you're comfortable with technology, have a reliable Internet connection, and want to pay bills as quickly as possible, consider paying online. Here are the steps you'll follow if you choose this option:

1. Receive paper bills via regular mail or bill-ready notifications via email.

2. For paper bills, open each bill and discard the outer and return envelopes. For e-bills, print the notice. Add the bills to others waiting to be paid.

3. If you don't already have a schedule for paying bills, create one: Consider when you will have money (your pay dates), when you have to give money away (the due dates on the bills), and your temperament (sprinter or jogger) to determine how often you must tend to this task; then write it into your calendar. You can also set up reminders in your software, but don't rely solely on this method because the reminders will work only when you're in the software!

4. On bill-paying day, gather your bills and sit down at the computer. Open your money-management software and log in to your bank's online banking Web site or each payee's online payment screen.

5. Create a payment for each bill in your online banking account or the vendor's Web site and set the pay date for each. Record each transaction in your money-management software. Use the report features in your software or your online banking system to create your "Did I Pay That?" document as needed.

> **caution** If you set up auto-debits, don't forget to record them. It's nauseating to get an overdraft notice due to a legitimate debit you set up and then forgot about.

6. File the printout or statement portion of the bill if you keep them. (You'll learn more about filing systems in Chapter 5.)

ELECTRONIC AND AUTOMATIC BILL-PAYING

If you're considering paying your bills in ways other than the old write-a-check-and-mail-it routine, it's important to know the difference between electronic bill-paying and automatic bill-paying.

Many companies now allow customers to pay their bills online or by phone via electronic funds transfer. This can mean using a credit card (you're probably used to that) or authorizing a debit from your checking account (a somewhat newer phenomenon). Many banks offer online bill-paying services, so you never have to write a check again.

The distinction to understand with any electronic transaction is whether you are sending the money or the payee is coming into your account and taking it. If you use a bank's bill-paying service, even if you authorize recurring payments to the same payee, each payment is issued by the bank to the payee and you control the date the payment is sent. If, on the other hand, you sign up for automatic bill payment through a company's Web site, the company then has the authority to come into your account and take its money—and many do not remove those funds exactly when they say they will. It could be a few days earlier, which could wreak havoc with your account management if you maintain a low balance.

Sticking with Your System

By now you've heard me say over and over how important it is to make your system work for you and not the other way around. You now have the best system you could possibly build for yourself with the information you have available to you right now. If, going forward, you find that something's not working the way you had hoped, change it! Don't get caught up in blaming yourself—refine your system until it's comfortable, efficient, and effective for you.

Remember that it takes time to change behaviors. We are creatures of habit, and that can work both for and against us. Give yourself a few months to transition through that awkward stage of moving from old habits to new. Do whatever works for you to remind yourself to keep on top of money management, whether it's writing your bill-paying days on your calendar, setting an alarm in your PDA, blanketing your space with sticky notes, or mentally attaching the task to another one that's already ingrained (for example, if you always remember to take out the trash, start paying the bills just before or after). If you keep at it, eventually your new system will become second nature.

A COMPLETELY PASSIVE BILL-PAYING OPTION

There is something you can do to make the entire bill-paying process go away: Pay someone else to do it.

For a fee, many accountants and even some banks offer bill-paying services that cover the whole process from start to finish: You change your billing address so your bills go to your bill-payer; they receive the bills, pay them from the account(s) you've designated, pay themselves the same way, and send you a summary once a month.

This premium service is not only for the wealthy. Those who travel extensively are often unable to retrieve their mail for weeks at a time, meaning bills would go unpaid without this assistance. And some folks are simply not able to get a grip on the money management process, or they spend many hours at it that could be put to more productive use. In these situations, a service like this is a better value or even a necessity, but certainly not a luxury.

If you're willing and able to pay for such a service (check around; it's not always as expensive as you might think) and you regularly have enough funds in your account to cover your bills, you can offload the chore of bill-paying onto someone else!

If, despite your best efforts, you still find yourself not using the system, give some more thought to why that might be. Is it truly as refined as it could be? If you're sure that the mechanics of the system are as good as you can make them but it's still not enough, consider consulting with a professional organizer who can evaluate your system with a fresh eye. Are you forcing yourself to do something that's really not your forte? Are there emotional issues that make this difficult for you? Consider talking to a therapist who can help you work through the thoughts and feelings that might be holding you back.

CHECK YOUR CREDIT

Now that you're avoiding late fees and overdrafts, you should also review your credit report for accuracy on a regular basis. Check in with each of the three reporting agencies:

* **Equifax**—800-685-1111 or www.equifax.com

* **Experian**—888-397-3742 or www.experian.com

* **TransUnion**—800-888-4213 or www.tuc.com

You should review your files with all three agencies; the information they have on you often varies.

If you visit their Web sites, poke around until you find the free or nearly free options: You can pay extra for immediate online access, enhanced reports that provide more information or a more readable format, combination reports that give you all three agencies' data plus your credit score, and services that promise to monitor your report and alert you if anything goes awry. These services are the ones displayed most prominently on the Web sites; just be aware that you can have a no-frills, yet complete, copy of your credit report mailed to you for $10 or less. Under some circumstances, for example, if you have been the victim of identity theft, the fee is often waived. Check each reporting agency's Web site for details.

Also know that the credit reporting agencies will sell your contact information to mailing lists; if you don't want them to, find their opt-out procedure and complete it.

If you do find an error or evidence of fraudulent activity in one of your reports, call the agency or go back to its Web site for instructions on what to do next.

Summary

That's one more huge step completed! Now you have a system for keeping up with the bills and avoiding the late fees and overdrafts of the past, so let's move on to the next chapter where you'll learn to surf the wave of incoming paper that will flow into your bill-paying system.

Part II

Corral the Paper

4   Fighting the Data Deluge...................... 65

5   Here to Stay: Storing Documents
    for Easy Retrieval 77

6   Proving It's Yours, Or Should Be 97

Fighting the Data Deluge

Ⓝo matter where we turn, we have incoming paper. Often it's mailed to us or arrives in the form of an email (which we might print) or a fax; it can be receipts we bring home from shopping or documents we acquire from insurance agents, investment advisors, realtors, decorators, or other consultants. Our kids bring it home from school, and it gets left on our doorstep (phone books and newspapers) or wedged into the screen (coupons or fliers from local businesses).

To keep your finances organized, it is imperative that all financial documents mixed in with the rest of the paper wave somehow are identified, separated, and moved into your financial management system. The best way to make sure nothing slips through the cracks is to formulate a plan for managing not just financial papers, but all papers.

Whoa. *That* sounds like a daunting task, doesn't it? It's true that paper management is a large, multifaceted, ongoing job. But, there is hope: If you put a system in place and maintain it regularly, you will be able to manage paper. Building that system does take a significant investment of time and energy, but it is absolutely worth the effort—the alternative is financial disarray, and we all know how much stress is caused by money trouble.

To control paper, you have to attend to its entire life cycle, which can be divided into three stages:

1. The point at which it enters your life
2. The time that it stays
3. The point at which it leaves

In this chapter:

❋ Managing the daily mail

❋ Dealing with other sources of incoming documents

❋ Handling documents that are pending, in progress, or waiting for a reply

❋ Passing on documents for others in your household

At each of these stages, you must make important decisions in a timely manner, and you must carry them out efficiently; otherwise, you will soon find yourself behind in your paperwork. Remember that episode of *I Love Lucy* where she's working the conveyor belt in a candy factory? Yeah, it's just like that, except you can't catch up on paperwork by eating the excess pages.

In previous chapters, you set up a system for capturing receipts, so you've already taken a big step in the management of your important data. But, as you know all too well, there is still a tsunami of paper yet to be conquered.

In this chapter you will learn ways to surf that wave of paper and finally exert control over it. You'll be ready to get your name removed from mailing lists, and you'll protect your identity with a shredding schedule. After you've completed the projects here, your mail will be manageable, you will know what to do with any incoming document, and you'll be ready to tackle what you need for the second and third stages of paper's life: a filing system.

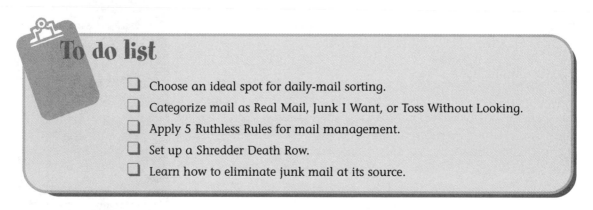

To do list

- ❑ Choose an ideal spot for daily-mail sorting.
- ❑ Categorize mail as Real Mail, Junk I Want, or Toss Without Looking.
- ❑ Apply 5 Ruthless Rules for mail management.
- ❑ Set up a Shredder Death Row.
- ❑ Learn how to eliminate junk mail at its source.

Incoming! Taking Control of Paper at the Point of Entry

We'll start with the biggest source of incoming household paper: the daily mail. Remember, the reason this matters is that you have to get to anything finance-related and move it over into your financial management system, so no matter how detailed you choose to be with the following projects, make sure your "money mail" is the top priority.

If paper management is a war, the daily mail delivery is a battle, and every item in your mailbox is The Enemy. Okay, maybe it's not that serious, but it's not something to be treated casually, either. If paper management was a no-brainer, thousands of professional organizers would be out of a job. So give this daily task the importance it requires with these ruthless rules for managing the mail:

Incoming mail

1. Get rid of the junk.
2. Put financial mail where it belongs.
3. Pass on others' mail.
4. Put magazines, catalogs, and packages where they belong.
5. Deal with the leftovers.

Read on for detailed battle plans.

You'll need list

❑ A trash can (at least 8-gallon) near the door that the mail comes in
❑ A shredder (optional, but strongly recommended)
❑ One container per family member (including yourself) to hold each person's mail
❑ A decorative container for magazines

Step 1: Get Rid of the Junk

One reason we end up with junk in our homes is that it wasn't junk when we acquired it. Things coming into our homes are either bright and shiny and immediately useful, or they have great potential: I'll fix it/read it/use it this summer/give it to my sister. These things might or might not become useless later, but for now I want them.

There is one exception, one thing that is unwanted, unneeded, a complete nuisance…and yet we bring it in almost every day of the week. It's the Grinch of incoming items, the vampire on the doorstep waiting for the invitation to come in and cause trouble. It's hated, it's demonized, it just won't give up: It's junk mail.

Weeding Out the Junk

Despite any efforts you might make to minimize junk mail, some unwanted items are bound to appear in your mailbox. The first step in tackling this problem is to decide what is "junk" to you. If it's unwanted and unneeded, it's junk. Bills might be unwanted, but you have to pay them, so they're not junk. You might think of catalogs or coupons as junk mail, but the ones you want aren't really junk. If you're not in the market for a new credit card, all credit card offers are junk.

You will also find junk and non-junk mixed together in the same mailing. The statement your investment company sends isn't junk, but if you never read prospectuses (those little booklets with detailed information on the companies you're invested in) and have no reason to keep them, they're junk. The same goes for newsletters that accompany utility bills or coupons that come with credit card statements. The key to making your mail management process efficient on a daily basis is to decide ahead of time, in broad categories, what you will toss and what you will keep. Create your own list or chart, or just decide on categories in your head, but categorize your mail and use your categories to quickly sort out the incoming mail you receive. Table 4.1, for example, shows a list I made of the kinds of "real," "good junk," and "junk junk" mail I receive. Table 4.1 shows just one example of things you might list in each of your mail categories. Make your own customized set of lists to breeze through your daily mail sort.

Table 4.1   Mail Categories

Real Mail	Junk Mail I Want	Toss without Looking
Bills	Ads from Kroger or Lowe's	Mail from banks I don't have accounts with
Bank statements	Levenger or Land's End catalogs	Prospectuses
Investment company statements	Pizza Hut coupons	Free or sample magazines, marketing newsletters, and so on
Time Magazine and *TV Guide*	Humane Society or Habitat for Humanity mailings	Any other ads
Packages I've ordered		Any other catalogs
Personal letters or greeting cards (with a real, recognizable return address)		Any other coupons
Book-of-the-Month Club packets		Any credit card or refinancing offers
Rent-by-mail DVDs		Mail from any other charity
		AOL discs
		Sweepstakes entries
		Any other mail addressed to Occupant, Resident, or The Single Person at

Every day when you get the mail, use your categories to quickly separate the wanted from the junk. Ideally, do your sort as close to the actual mailbox as you can and have a wastebasket within tossing distance. I wish I could keep a trash can right under my mailbox, but the weather around here often precludes sorting the mail outside. Instead, I have one in a cabinet in my front room; if the cabinet wasn't there, I'd use the coat closet just inside the front door.

caution
Don't sit down while you sort your mail. If you stand, you'll breeze through it more quickly. Be disciplined—don't waste time flipping through catalogs that aren't on your Junk Mail I Want list, and don't feel obligated to open mailings from charities just because they sent you free address labels.

I grab the mailbox contents, take three steps into the living room, open the cabinet door, and toss an average of 90% of the day's mail before it has a chance to infiltrate my home. Then I close the cabinet and strut away, savoring my daily victory. You, too, can enjoy this smug satisfaction.

TAKE ME OFF YOUR LIST!

Want to reduce junk mail coming to your home? Follow any or all of these steps:

* **Write to the Direct Marketing Association's Mail Preference Service to be added to its name-removal file—**Use the online form at www.dmaconsumers.org/cgi/offmailinglist#regform (see Figure 4.1; $5 to submit electronically, or just print and mail it), or send a letter with your full name, complete home address, telephone number, and signature to

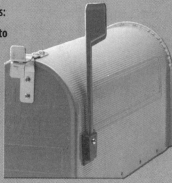

    DMA Mail Preference Service
    Box 643
    Carmel, NY 10512

    Your listing will take effect within three months (lists are distributed to vendors quarterly) and will remain valid for five years.

    Note that this will not completely eliminate junk mail. Companies are not required to use MPS to purge their mailing lists, so you will still receive mail from those who do not participate in this voluntary program. You will also receive mail from companies with which you do business, unless you instruct them individually to place you on their do-not-mail list. Visit the Consumer FAQs section of the DMA Web site (www.dmaconsumers.org) for more information on minimizing mail, email, and phone solicitations and protecting your privacy as a consumer.

FIGURE 4.1

The Direct Marketing Association's Mail Preference Service can help you remove yourself from mailing lists. Visit www. dmaconsumers. org for instructions.

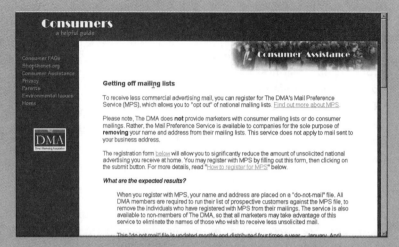

Consumers
a helpful guide

Consumer FAQs
Shoptheret.org
Consumer Assistance
Privacy
Parents
Environmental Issues
Home

Consumer Assistance

Getting off mailing lists

To receive less commercial advertising mail, you can register for The DMA's Mail Preference Service (MPS), which allows you to "opt out" of national mailing lists. Find out more about MPS.

Please note, The DMA does **not** provide marketers with consumer mailing lists or do consumer mailings. Rather, the Mail Preference Service is available to companies for the sole purpose of **removing** your name and address from their mailing lists. This service does not apply to mail sent to your business address.

The registration form below will allow you to significantly reduce the amount of unsolicited national advertising you receive at home. You may register with MPS by filling out this form, then clicking on the submit button. For more details, read "How to register for MPS" below.

What are the expected results?

When you register with MPS, your name and address are placed on a "do-not-mail" file. All DMA members are required to run their list of prospective customers against the MPS file, to remove the individuals who have registered with MPS from their mailings. The service is also available to non-members of The DMA, so that all marketers may take advantage of this service to eliminate the names of those who wish to receive less unsolicited mail.

This "do-not-mail" file is updated monthly and distributed four times a year — January, April

✳ **Eliminate all magazine subscriptions**—Or you can contact each and say, "You are not authorized to rent or share my name and contact information with anyone." Look for a customer service phone number in the magazine's staff list, or check its Web site for instructions on how to opt out of third-party mailings.

✳ **Do not enter sweepstakes offers that arrive in the mail.**

✳ **Contact the National Opt-Out Center at 888-5OPT-OUT (888-567-8688)**—You can stop unwanted credit card offers by removing your name from the marketing lists of the three major credit bureaus: Equifax, Experian (formerly TRW), and TransUnion.

✳ **Complete the U.S. Postal Service's Form 1500**—This will prevent sexually oriented advertising (SOA) from being mailed to you or your children. The form is available from your local post office or as a downloadable document on the USPS Web site at www.usps.com/forms/pdf/ps1500.pdf.

✳ **Get in the habit of telling every vendor to keep you off its marketing lists**—You'll be saying it a lot: Every time you open a new credit card account, make an online or telephone purchase, order from a catalog, make a charitable donation, or even make a purchase in a store. If you're serious about minimizing unwanted mail, you have to speak up every time you share your contact information.

If you prefer to shred things like credit card offers or anything that might contain your contact information, have a shredder ready to use in each day's mail culling (see the later section, "Be a Super Shredder").

Trashing the Bad That Comes with the Good

You'll eliminate most of the junk mail with your initial sort, but when you open the "good" mail, you'll often find still more stuff to toss. I like to get rid of all of it as soon as it comes in and transfer only the relevant parts of the mailing to their designated places in my home. Some people don't like to open mail until they're ready to deal with it, and that's fine. Either way, be ready to ditch the junk once the envelope is opened. Envelope stuffers that you probably don't need include

- **Mini-newsletters that come with utility bills or investment statements**—Skim the newsletter for important information and, if you find some, tear that part out and ditch the rest.
- **Coupons or ad slips that come with credit card bills**—I never even consider them; if I'm getting a credit card bill, I definitely don't need the company's featured figurine or pen set.
- **Catalogs and ad packets that come in the box with items you've ordered.**
- **Parts of a catalog or magazine that don't interest you**—Some people relax by kicking back with their magazines and catalogs and really savoring each page. If that's not you, flip through them as they come in, tear out only the parts you want to read or consider, and toss the rest right then and there.
- **Outer envelopes**—Just stick the bill inside the payment envelope to keep them together.

There. You've tossed most of what came in the mail today. Now, what to do with what's left?

Be a Super Shredder

They're not just for offices any more: Keep a shredder next to your kitchen trash can (if you have a disposal, there might be an extra outlet available under the sink). Choose a confetti-cut model for extra security, and for extra convenience, make it one that can take many sheets at once and can shred plastic, so you can feed it unopened credit card offers—envelope, letter, and fake card all together (see Figure 4.2).

FIGURE 4.2

A shredder to consider: the Fellowes PS60C-2 (www. fellowes.com; suggested retail $161.99) shreds eight sheets at a time into 5/32" × 1 3/8" particles and can handle credit cards, staples, and paper clips.

With a powerful new shredder, you might find yourself looking for things to shred. Yes, it's fun, but don't get carried away and shred a document before its time. Instead, set up a Shredder Death Row for documents you're keeping only until they clear your accounts, such as ATM slips, check carbons, and receipts you don't need to save. Here's how to do it:

1. Create three files or containers labeled This Month, Last Month, and Two Months Ago, and make room for them within easy reach of where you do your paperwork, or near your shredder (or, ideally, both).

2. After you've entered your transactions into your financial tracking system, file the receipts that will eventually be shredded in This Month.

3. At the start of the new month, move the contents of This Month to Last Month and start filing new items in This Month. A month later, move everything forward: Last Month goes to Two Months Ago, and This Month goes to Last Month. A month after that, shred the contents of Two Months Ago and move the other two forward once again.

4. With each new month, dispense with the Two Months Ago items and move the rest one step closer to The End.

Now you don't have to recheck the date on each little slip of paper to decide when it meets its doom. If you're keeping up with balancing your accounts, if there isn't anything that's still waiting to clear from two months ago, and if you don't have any purchases to return or dispute from two months ago, you can shred everything in your Two Months Ago file without reevaluating it.

One thing to keep in mind as you feed one document after another into your shredder is that shredders intended for household use get tired rather quickly, so be sure to use yours no more than the manufacturer's recommended run time per day. If you don't know what that amount of time is for your shredder, a reasonable guideline is no more than 5 minutes at a time.

note Remember: If you don't keep up with the daily paper onslaught, you will soon be buried in it.

Step 2: Put Financial Mail Where It Belongs

If you've completed Chapter 1, "Tracking Your Money," you already have a designated place for receipts, ATM slips, and the like. Now, expand that to include a place for incoming bills and account statements. It can be the same place or somewhere else—just make sure it's convenient and safe from pets, kids, and other perils. Ideally it will be a container, shelf, drawer, or file near where you manage your finances. What matters is that it works for you and that you use it consistently.

Every day when you sort the mail, transfer the bills, statements, and other financial mail to this designated spot so it's ready to process the next time you update your finances.

Step 3: Pass on Others' Mail

If personal mail for another household member is in the day's delivery, put it in its designated spot. And where would that be, you ask? Time to create another home: Choose a spot where others can expect to find their mail, if they have any. As the designated mail sorter, be sure you put their mail in that spot every time so they won't have an excuse to bring in the mail themselves and mess up your system!

Step 4: Put Magazines, Catalogs, and Packages Where They Belong

Take the day's magazines and catalogs to their designated spot. (If you need to create another home, now's the time.) Your best bet is a container of a manageable size (say, 1 cubic foot at most) that complements the decor of the room where you will read these materials. It might be a basket, a decorative metal bin, an ottoman with storage, or a drawer in a coffee table. When the container becomes full, it's time to purge some publications, even though you haven't read them yet!

If something you ordered came in with the day's mail, you don't need me to tell you what to do with it: That's like getting a present! Well, okay, maybe a little advice: Open it, take out the item and make sure you love it (try it on if needed), add the packing slip or receipt to your financial mail, and then toss the packaging.

tip If you're not one to sit down and savor a magazine, just tear out the articles that interest you during your daily mail sort and scrap the rest.

Step 5: Deal with the Leftovers

There will be many days when your mail management process ends with step 4. In fact, you will probably have some days that are all step 1! Once in a while, though, you will receive something other than the stuff in steps 1–4. Here's hoping it's something good (happy birthday).

When you receive something in the mail that doesn't fit the parameters of the previous steps, follow this basic organizing rule and do one of three things:

- **File it**—It might just be something informational, like a membership directory for a group to which you belong. Anything that doesn't require action on your part but contains information you want to keep should be filed or otherwise put away.

- **Act on it**—It might be a letter notifying you of a problem, such as a note from the city ordering you to have that crack in your sidewalk repaired. Anything that requires you to follow up, take action, or respond in some way should be added to your to-do system.

- **Toss it**—It might be something that seemed important, but upon closer inspection turns out to be nothing you need. You know what to do: Get rid of it!

Now you have a five-step plan of attack for managing the daily mail. With practice, this will become a 5-minute process, and you'll be that much closer to winning the war against incoming paper.

What about Incoming Paper from Other Sources?

It's not just the mail carrier who brings you paperwork. It might be your spouse, kids, parents, or friends, and often you bring it in yourself. The easiest way to handle this paper is to add it to your daily mail processing. Follow the same steps—toss the junk, put the financial documents and reading materials where they belong, and deal with the rest using the File/Act/Toss model.

Paperwork from Others in Your Household

Sometimes you won't be there for the others to hand you their papers. Choose a drop-off spot for them to use (your desk, a container on the kitchen counter, your pillow—whatever works for you) and coach them to use it every time. Do your part by regularly checking the drop-off spot for papers that need your attention.

For sign-and-return documents—school permission slips, applications that require both spouse's signatures, and so on—decide where you will leave the papers after they're signed. You could put them back in the same drop-off spot or put them in the place designated for incoming mail for each person. Again, be consistent: Make these systems and use them every time so they become habits.

Dealing with Odds and Ends

These guidelines will help you address the great majority of your incoming paper-work. But, of course, every household is different, so there will probably be some form of paper not discussed here that you will have to fit into your system. Don't let those oddball items defeat you! Add a step to your mail-management system, or set up a separate container for the misfit category—do anything that makes sense for you. Just make sure you deal with that odd document—one way or another, make a decision about it.

Over and over again, my clients find that it's the last 10% of the loose paper that's hardest to address. Don't let that small percentage continue to float around—take a deep breath and power through it!

Summary

Whew! Doesn't that feel better? Now all your incoming papers have places to go, and you have systems for deciding what to do with them no matter what their purpose, value, or stage of life. But I know what you're thinking: You also have a big (okay, huge) pile called To Be Filed, and it's growing every day! Quick, move on to Chapter 5, "Here to Stay: Storing Documents for Easy Retrieval," and knock that pile down to size.

Here to Stay: Storing Documents for Easy Retrieval

No matter how adept you are at discarding documents the moment they become unneeded, there will still be a certain amount of paper in your life. It's a necessary evil. Luckily, you can contain it and thereby minimize its disruptive impact on your peace of mind and every horizontal surface in your home.

As with everything else you own, if a document is worth keeping, it's worth giving it a home within your home—a place where it belongs. We all know important documents are useless if they can't be found when they're needed—that's why miscellaneous paper piles cause us so much anxiety!

In this chapter, you learn what to do with those financial papers that are here for the duration. You create storage systems to make your documents easy to retrieve when you need them, and you make them your way: files, piles, or a little of both, with sections and categories that make sense to *you*. And here's a bonus: The principles in this chapter can also be applied to your nonfinancial document storage!

In this chapter:

* Reviewing your paper storage options
* Creating a filing system for financial documents
* Choosing a method for dealing with papers in transition
* Following a plan for going paperless

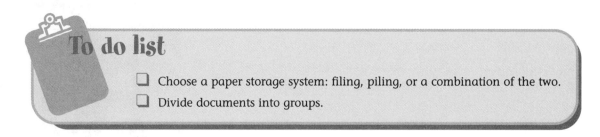

To do list

❑ Choose a paper storage system: filing, piling, or a combination of the two.

❑ Divide documents into groups.

File or Pile? Choosing Paper Storage Options

You are now at a crossroads much like the scene in Figure 5.1, and you must choose one road or the other before continuing on to set up your filing system. To the right is the far more common route, a veritable four-lane highway of paper management. To the left, a humble footpath—most definitely the road less traveled of organized paper storage.

FIGURE 5.1

Which paper storage path is right for you?

Traditional, vertical, in-cabinet filing is the correct choice for many people. It's efficient, aesthetically pleasing, logical, and universally recognizable.

But let's not dismiss the left-hand path too quickly. True, it's not often used effectively, and most people who attempt it don't know that it can be a legitimate solution. However, for some, that less-traveled road—horizontal, in-sight piling instead of filing—really is the best way to go.

You'll need list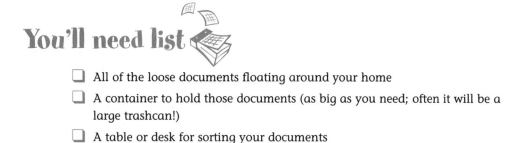

- [ ] All of the loose documents floating around your home
- [ ] A container to hold those documents (as big as you need; often it will be a large trashcan!)
- [ ] A table or desk for sorting your documents

Piling Might Be Right

If you have never had a problem with filing, don't mind filing, absolutely *love* filing, the choice is simple—you can move forward to "Step 1: Divide Your Documents into Groups." But if you tend to have piles of paper—even if you also have files and even if you're perpetually working on ridding yourself of those piles—perhaps you should stop resisting and actually embrace a piling system.

Some reasons that piling might be for you:

- You believe you will lose things if they're put away. For you, they truly will be "out of sight, out of mind."

- You find it easiest to retrieve documents based on their color or shape as you look at the side of a stack of papers.

- You can't seem to think in categories when they're inside a file cabinet, but you can and do apply categories to your piles.

- You are able to find what you need from a pile in a reasonable amount of time (say, within two minutes).

- You have enough horizontal surfaces (countertops, shelves, and so on) to accommodate your paper piles without resorting to piling on the floor, and no one will pitch a fit if you keep a bunch of paper stacks sitting out.

If this sounds like you, consider using piles instead of files as you complete the projects in this chapter. Take care to make your piles distinctive from one another (use the principles of grouping and categorizing you'll learn next), and keep them neat enough that they won't fall over and get mixed together (large rubber bands can help with this). You might also find it useful to top each pile with a cover sheet naming its contents.

If piling appeals to you, give it a try: If it doesn't work, you can always go with a more conventional system instead.

The Best of Both Worlds

If full-blown piling is not practical for you, you can compromise with a hybrid system: documents in file folders, but stored in sight in vertical holders instead of file drawers. This turned out to be the ideal system for one of my clients, a very busy and successful business owner named Nick.

Nick absolutely hates file cabinets. He considers them useful only for dead files—archives that will probably never be needed again. He would never dream of putting an active client file in a file cabinet—that would be the same as killing the deal. Instead, he creates a file folder for each active job, using third-cut manila folders in various colors. The colors don't represent anything (in other words, red doesn't mean urgent), but whatever color he happens to choose for each job sticks in his memory, so when he looks for that file he remembers he's looking for a certain color as well. He writes the job name on the tab at the top and keeps everything to do with that job in one folder. If it gets too big, he adds a second folder (yes, of the same color) and keeps them together.

And where does he keep these folders? In vertical inclined file racks, similar to the one shown in Figure 5.2, that hold files in a stair-step pattern, so each file name is visible. Nick has dozens of jobs in progress at any given time, so he has about 8–10 file racks on the surfaces around his desk. The result is that his office resembles a football stadium: He's surrounded by ascending rows of seats, each of which holds a person he recognizes, and he's the quarterback in the center of the field.

FIGURE 5.2

Vertical inclined file racks, such as this one made by Staples and available from www.staples.com, enable you to file without putting papers out of sight, out of mind.

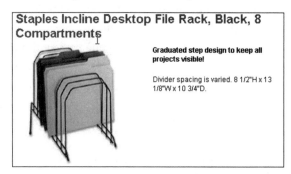

Staples Incline Desktop File Rack, Black, 8 Compartments

Graduated step design to keep all projects visible!

Divider spacing is varied. 8 1/2"H x 13 1/8"W x 10 3/4"D.

For an out-of-sight-out-of-mind person, this arrangement provides much comfort and a great deal of power: Everything Nick needs is within reach, safe from loss, and ready to be used, and for him, this is an effective system. For a person prone to visual overload, however, it would be a distracting, discordant, Crayola-bright nightmare.

For another in-sight filing option, think of the doctor's office. If you've ever gazed with appreciation at that wall of patient records—all those folders lined up on a shelf, with neat little stickers on the edge, so nice and tidy—perhaps you'd like to apply the same system at home. All you need is a supply of end tab folders (see Figure 5.3), some bookends, and some open shelf space. Write your file name on the longer, right edge of the folder instead of the top, and you'll be able to store and retrieve your files easily and in plain sight—no drawers needed.

FIGURE 5.3

End-tab folders, such as these made by Oxford and available at www.staples.com, allow you to file on a shelf, like they do in a doctor's office.

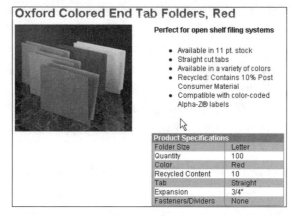

Oxford Colored End Tab Folders, Red

Perfect for open shelf filing systems

- Available in 11 pt. stock
- Straight cut tabs
- Available in a variety of colors
- Recycled: Contains 10% Post Consumer Material
- Compatible with color-coded Alpha-Z® labels

Product Specifications	
Folder Size	Letter
Quantity	100
Color	Red
Recycled Content	10
Tab	Straight
Expansion	3/4"
Fasteners/Dividers	None

Have you decided whether to file, pile, or combine the two? If so, you're ready for the first round of paper-taming: dividing into groups.

GO (MOSTLY) PAPERLESS

If you're in favor of eliminating paper, comfortable with your computer and scanner, and don't mind adding a few minutes to your filing routine, consider going paperless with your household record-keeping.

Instead of filing paper documents in actual file folders, you scan each document into your computer to create an electronic record of it; then you file that record in a subfolder within your computer. Create your filing categories as explained later, but do so on your computer's hard drive instead of in a traditional file cabinet. When you receive paper documents that need filing, scan each one, give it a meaningful name (for example, Electric Bill June 2004), and save it to the appropriate computer folder.

Here are some caveats:

❋ Make absolutely sure that your computer is safe from hackers and snoops. If you have any concerns that someone could access your data, store your files on CD-ROM or use traditional paper files.

❋ If you don't already have a scanner, consider carefully whether the expense and the learning process to become adept with it will pay off for you.

✳ If you choose electronic document storage, take extra care to back up your computer files frequently.

✳ Be sure to scan and save your documents in a format that is legible, easy to access, and allows you to reprint them if necessary.

✳ Consider the amount of space your electronic files will take up on your hard drive. Remember that .bmp files are considerably larger than .jpg, so choose wisely when you select the format in which to save your records.

✳ Note that there will always be some things for which you should keep the original paper copy—for example, birth certificates, Social Security cards, and passports.

✳ Rest assured that electronic documents are as good as the real thing in the eyes of the IRS, as long as they are legible, accurate, and complete.

Step 1: Divide Your Documents into Groups

The first thing you're going to do with those loose papers is separate them into groups. With this step, you can begin at the very beginning, working with those thoroughly miscellaneous loose papers you collected from your desk, floor, counter-top, bed, and of course the tops of the file cabinets! If you already have a partial file system, you can build around your existing files using the principles you learn here, or you can start from scratch. Your choice will probably depend on how well your old system has worked for you and much time you have to devote to this chapter. Remember the concept of Organized Enough as you decide whether to work around what you have or start fresh.

There are a few broad groups of files that I've found work well for most of my clients. These groups cover all of the paper storage needs of a typical household and are often housed in different areas of the home depending on how often they are accessed and how much prime file space is available. In a traditional filing system, you might have one group in each drawer; for a piling or hybrid system, you might arrange them with one group per shelf.

The file groups that I recommend are

- **Frequent Files**—These are the files you'll be using every time you pay bills or balance your accounts. If you prefer, call them Active Files or Daily Files.

- **Household**—These are accessed less often than Frequent Files but often enough that they should be housed in a convenient spot. These files might include medical records, kids' school records, pet records, local carryout menus and pizza coupons, or schedules for seasonal events like kids' soccer games or plays at your community theater.

- **Projects and Research**—These files are for special interests for which you tend to accumulate a fair amount of paper. This could include hobbies (for example, a Knitting file might contain patterns, pictures from magazines, diagrams of stitches, and yarn suppliers), medical concerns (for example, if you have diabetes, you might have some research printed out from the Internet, magazine articles, special dietary instructions, or guidelines for insulin usage), or world issues of interest to you (for example, global warming or the state of affairs in Israel). This is also the place for projects such as house-hunting, redecorating, or research toward buying a vehicle. Project files and Research files are often closely related, so it makes sense to keep them together.

- **Room by Room System**—This includes paperwork related to your belongings, including receipts, warranties, and instruction manuals. You get to build a set of Room by Room files in the next chapter.

- **Archives**—These are documents you don't expect to need any more, but that you want or need to keep for a period of time before you can dispose of them. The most common example in this group is tax returns; some people also save notes on problems they've had with a utility company or disputed insurance claims. Archive files can be stored in the least accessible, most inconvenient space in your home, or even in an offsite storage facility. They can also be categorized much more broadly than active files because they are the least likely of all to be accessed again. Some archive files are kept temporarily and others are permanent.

- **Safe Storage**—These are items from any of the other categories that are irreplaceable or especially precious to you. This could include family photos, love letters, or (in my case) demo tapes from an old friend's long-defunct rock band. The items in this group belong in a safety deposit box or in a fire safe with a rating appropriate for the type of media being stored.

This chapter focuses on Frequent Files and covers Archives and Safe Storage. In the next chapter, you learn how a set of Room by Room files can help you create a property inventory. After you've finished organizing your personal finances, you can use the techniques you've learned here to build your Household and Project/Research file groups and get rid of those remaining piles!

Sorting Out Documents for Frequent Files

The first and, for our purposes, most important group of files is what I call Frequent Files. Frequent Files include documents related to

- Bill-paying
- Financial accounts, including investments
- Income and expenses

Start a list of everything you can think of that fits this category for you. You can take a shortcut by listing every recurring expense and income category you identified in Chapter 1, "Tracking Your Money." Also list each of your banking and investment accounts.

As you make your list, rummage through that big pile of loose papers. You'll probably find documents you hadn't thought of ("Oh yeah, the darn property taxes!"); add them to your list. As you rummage, separate Frequent File documents from the rest of pile. This step will feel good—this is the point at which most people think, "Finally, I'm making some progress!"

If you're thinking ahead, you might find yourself trying to separate recent Frequent Files from old ones, anticipating that the aged Frequent File items will go into the Archive group. You are correct! You can make this further separation now or later, whichever you prefer.

By the time you've weeded the entire pile for Frequent File items, your Frequent File list will be complete and you'll be ready to make your folders.

Setting Aside Other Groups

Now you have a pile of Frequent Files contents, a list of everything you can think of that will go into Frequent Files, and a big messy pile of everything else. That "everything else" pile is made up of documents that fit into the other major file groups (Household, Research/Projects, Room by Room, Archives, and Safe Storage). Leave these for now; we'll come back to the pile and extract more groups in a little while. Throw that random pile back into the container you used to gather it, put a lid on it so you don't have to look at it, and focus on the next step for your Frequent Files.

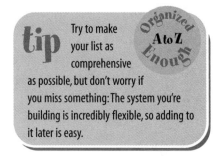

tip Try to make your list as comprehensive as possible, but don't worry if you miss something: The system you're building is incredibly flexible, so adding to it later is easy.

CREATE A PAUSE PLACE FOR PAPER

Now you know what to do with paper when it comes in and how to settle it in to stay for a while. But what about those in-between papers: Can't toss it yet, but won't need it long enough to file it?

Typical pending items that tend to float around on the kitchen counter, in a junk drawer, or on the fridge door include

- ❋ Printouts of online orders not yet received
- ❋ Raffle tickets
- ❋ Notes on messages you've left and are waiting for replies
- ❋ Papers you'll need to take with you in the next few days
- ❋ Coupons
- ❋ Shopping lists
- ❋ Receipts for items to be returned
- ❋ Prescriptions

Create one comprehensive system for dealing with these floaters, or make a series of smaller systems. Some examples are listed here:

- ❋ Use a clipboard tucked into the front hall closet to hold order confirmations. When the package arrives, remove the corresponding confirmation slip from the clipboard. If the clipboard is empty, there's nothing pending.
- ❋ Designate a section of your wallet for coupons, prescriptions, and receipts for returns. Note these items on your shopping list so you'll remember to use them.
- ❋ Tape your shopping list inside a kitchen cabinet door so everyone can add to it as needed. Some people tape their coupons and prescriptions to the shopping list so they remember to use them.
- ❋ Keep a file folder in your vehicle to hold any out-of-the-ordinary documents you'll need to take with you in the near future.
- ❋ If you would prefer one big system for all these items, create a *tickler* file. Label 31 folders 1–31, and label an additional 12 folders with each month, January–December. Use the numbered files for the days of the current month and each month's folder for future months. File every pending item in the day on which you need to attend to it or expect to receive a reply or shipment. Every day—*every day!*—check the appropriate folder for pending items.

A Quick Lesson in Categorizing

Now that you have your Frequent Files group, you can apply a greater level of order by creating categories within the group. But first, some background information. There are three principles I want you to understand about categorization.

Categorizing Is Better Than Alphabetizing

This concept makes many of my clients exclaim, "Why didn't I think of that? That's so obvious, and such an improvement!" Simply put: It's filing by category instead of alphabetically. Look at Figure 5.4 for a comparison. The beauty of categorizing instead of alphabetizing is that it relies on your logic, not your memory.

FIGURE 5.4

When filing, the alphabet can't do it all. For a really useful system, use categories such as those in the system on the right. Notice the positioning of the file tabs: The first position is a main category; the second position indicates a subcategory of the first; a tab in the third position means the file is a subset of the one in the second position, and so on.

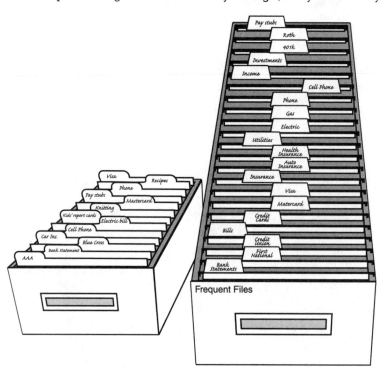

You might not realize it, but with an alphabetical system, it's not the alphabet that's doing the work for you—it's your own memory. You have to remember whether you filed Angie's report card under *A* for Angie, *R* for report cards, or *S* for school.

If you build a categorized file system using your own logic, you could leave that system untouched for a year, and when you come back to it and look at the file tabs, it will still make sense to you. The system must be built around *your* logic—not mine or another organizer's or your mom's—because no matter how sound another person's logic is, it's not exactly the way *your* mind works.

Think in Terms of "Which Is Bigger?"

When you file by category instead of alphabetically, you can use subcategories much more effectively. For example, look at how I categorized *Cell phone* in Figure 5.4. In the alphabetical system, it's under *C* for cell phone, but it could just have easily been under *P* for phone, mixed in with the landline phone bills, or I could have also named it Verizon cellular and filed it under *V*.

In the categorized system, Cell phone is a subset of Phone, which is a subset of Utilities, which is a subset of Bills. Logic allows me to start with Bills and drill down to the item I want; the alphabet requires me to guess which of several equally valid names might have been used.

By the way, are you thinking, "Why would she put Phone under Utilities?" Good! I think of phones as a form of household utility, but many people do not. That's why my system is great for me, and yours must match the way you think!

The ability to use subcategories gives you much more power when you build your Frequent Files, but it can also lead to a dilemma: Which will be the main category and which will be the subcategory? I think of this as the "which is bigger?" problem—not physically larger, but conceptually or functionally.

For example, take car insurance. Would you make Insurance a subset of Car, or would you make Car a subset of Insurance? Which is a bigger category to you—everything car-related or all types of insurance? If Insurance is bigger, then you'll have Insurance as a main category, with subcategories such as Car, Health, House, and Life. If Car is bigger, your main category will be Car, with subcategories including Insurance and Maintenance.

Use Your Own Words

I can't stress this enough: You must name your files in language that makes sense to you! You do not have to—in fact, you shouldn't—make your system fit whatever words might be preprinted on your file folder tabs, or even the file names you see here. I've helped many a client to build a filing system, and every one of those systems turns out differently because I make sure that the files are named in the client's own words.

If you say *car* instead of *auto*, use *car* on your files. If you think *Web* instead of *Internet*, go with *Web*. You must name your files with the words you normally use; if you don't, your file system will always be unfamiliar to you.

note You must name your files with the words you normally use; if you don't, your file system will always be unfamiliar to you.

Keeping Categories Under Control

By now, you probably have some idea of how you want to categorize your Frequent Files, so you're almost ready to get started! Here's just one more thing to keep in mind as you draw up your categories and subcategories:

Use no more than five layers of subcategorization in your system. For example, in the category of Bills, you could have the subcategory Insurance, with a subcategory of Health Insurance, further divided into Doctor Visits, which in turn has a subcategory of Receipts. Don't go any more detailed than that (this example is even a bit too specific for my taste).

I recommend this limit for two reasons. First, if you break down your categories into more than five levels of detail, your system will most likely become more organized than it needs to be. Second, it will cause trouble when you create your file tabs in the next section. I'm betting you're really going to like the way we'll assemble these files, and to do it right, we need no more than five levels of subcategorization.

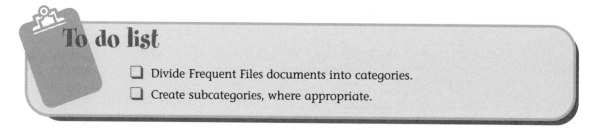

To do list

❏ Divide Frequent Files documents into categories.
❏ Create subcategories, where appropriate.

Step 2: Subdivide Your Frequent Files Group into Categories

Now you know to categorize whenever possible, understand how to think in terms of "which is bigger?," and are ready to name your categories and files in your own words. Let's apply these principles to your stack of Frequent Files documents.

You'll need list

❏ Frequent Files documents
❏ Lined paper for making lists (or use your computer!)

If you already have a filing system for documents like these and want to build around it, pretend for the moment that you are starting from scratch. Give yourself the freedom to develop a completely new system, unencumbered by the need to make your old and new systems cooperate. In reality, you probably will be able to fit your existing files into a new, more comprehensive system (perhaps the old files will just need new names), but if not, don't let your existing system limit your options here.

I recommend that you list all of your files on paper before you start creating the folders. This way, you can move them around, rename them, delete them if needed, and get the entire system planned out with the ideal level of detail and without wasting supplies and time.

Look once more at Figure 5.4. The set of files on the right is a good example of categorized Frequent Files. Refer to this example as you complete your list of Frequent Files categories. Remember to use your own language to name your categories!

You might notice that in subcategories containing more than one item, those items are alphabetized. You can choose whether you arrange the items within your subcategories by alphabetical order, chronological order (for example, arranging family members by age), or some other order that makes sense to you.

ANOTHER OPTION: FILING BY MONTH

And now for the opposite perspective, courtesy of Christine, another business owner and client of mine: If categorizing your Frequent Files, particularly those bills and statements that recur each month, seems too detailed for you, you could simply file them all by month. It will take you longer to find something if you need it, but if the alternative is that you'll never get around to filing, a simple by-month system is far better than nothing. It also makes archiving at the end of the year incredibly easy.

To do list

- ❑ Label folders for Frequent Files.
- ❑ Put those papers away!

Step 3: Label Your Folders and Start Filing!

Grab that Sharpie marker—it's time to write out your file folder tabs!

You have your list of Frequent Files categories; you also need a supply of hanging file folders, including the little plastic tabs that go with the folders and the paper inserts for those tabs. Notice that we're using only hanging file folders, not the interior kind where the tab is part of the folder. The reason is simple: You can't reposition the tabs on manila folders; on hanging files you can move the tab without switching the folder, and you need this flexibility to represent your subcategories correctly and adjust your system in the future.

You'll need list

❑ Your list of groups and categories

❑ Hanging file folders and tabs

❑ File drawers or containers

❑ A Sharpie marker or other thick-tipped pen for creating labels

And yes, I said you need a *marker* for making those tabs. I've found that many clients use pencil for this task, and I think it's because they're not confident that they're doing this correctly and want to be able to erase. To you, I say, "You're doing it right!" If you misspell, try again on the other side of the tab. And a Sharpie marker or thick pen is much easier to read, so no pencils, please.

And no labelers either! Unless you are absolutely sure that you will never skip making a new file because you don't feel like making a label or because you're out of label tape or batteries, I strongly recommend that you keep it simple and write your tabs by hand.

A Neat Trick with Hanging Folders

Check out the file folder tabs in Figure 5.4. Notice that the first tab, Bank Statements, is all the way to the left. This indicates that it's a main category. The tab for the next folder, First National, appears in the second position, meaning it is a subcategory of Bank Statements.

Look at the folders labeled Bills, Credit Cards, and MasterCard. Do you see that MasterCard is a subset of Credit Cards, which is a subset of Bills? Now you've got the idea!

There are 11 tab slots on the inside edge of a hanging file folder, and a standard tab occupies the space of 3 of those slots. This configuration creates 5 possible tab spaces (see Figure 5.5)—just right for five levels of categorization text.

FIGURE 5.5

There are 11 tab slots on the inside edges of a standard hanging file folder. This allows room for 5 hierarchical tab positions.

Filing Your Documents

After you've written out all of your tabs, place them in their spaces on the hanging files: Main categories in the first position, subcategories in the second, subcategories of those in the third, and so on. Drop your folders into their drawer or container, and you're ready to file!

As you work your way through your stack of Frequent Files, file each document in the most specific subcategory you can. This might mean that some of your first- or second-level folders actually remain empty: Sometimes they simply serve as placeholders in your system.

> **tip**
> Attach the file folder tab to the inside of the front edge of the folder, not the back. This makes it easier to pull the folder open—just grab the tab!

For example, you might have a Finance folder in the first position; one labeled Insurance in the second; and three folders for Homeowners, Life, and Medical in the third. The Insurance subcategory groups all of your insurances together, but that folder itself should only contain documents that are more general than any one of its three subcategories. Therefore, you might choose to file general articles about insurance in the Insurance folder, or you might just leave it empty.

As you're filing, don't worry if you haven't yet found every item for a category (for example, all 12 of last year's bank statements) and don't spend time now arranging the contents of each folder in order by date. Just getting the papers into the correct folder is plenty of progress; you can go back later and put them in date order if you want to. In fact, when you complete step 4 (whether now or down the road), you can accomplish two things at once: You can build your Archive files and put your current Frequent Files in chronological order at the same time.

To do list

- [ ] Pull Frequent File documents more than a year old.
- [ ] Set aside shreddables.
- [ ] Sort the remaining documents by year.
- [ ] Divide to-be-archived documents into permanent, temporary, and safe storage piles.

Step 4: Create Archive Files

You're ready to create your archives! Basically, financial archives are the documents within your Frequent Files that you need or want to keep for more than one calendar year. Whether it has been an hour or a year since you built your Frequent Files, this process is pretty simple. Archives don't need to be categorized like the rest of your files; they can simply be stored by year. I just lump everything together into one year: I would rather have to spend more time looking for something if I happen to need it later than spend extra time up-front arranging files that I will probably never need again.

note This step is optional for now. Translation: You probably have dozens of other tasks awaiting your attention, so if you want to move to the next chapter now, go ahead—your financial paperwork is now officially Organized Enough! You can come back later to create your archives.

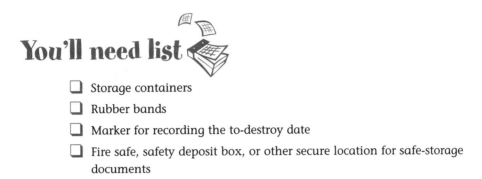

You'll need list

- ❏ Storage containers
- ❏ Rubber bands
- ❏ Marker for recording the to-destroy date
- ❏ Fire safe, safety deposit box, or other secure location for safe-storage documents

Separating Documents for Archiving

Now, go back through your Frequent Files folders and take out documents that are older than the current calendar year. As you work, make a stack of documents you need to archive and another stack of those to be shredded.

What should you archive? Anything that is tax-related; anything you need to save for legal purposes; anything you want to save for your own reference, such as utility bills. In general, archive anything you want or need to save, whether permanently or temporarily. Temporary archives are often never accessed again until it's time to destroy them. Permanent archives might never be accessed either: They're just documents you have to keep.

After you've gone through all of your Frequent Files, you'll have a stack of items to archive and a stack to shred. Set those shredder-destined papers aside and get rid of them with your next batch of shredding. Now, consider the stack to be archived.

Separate your archive documents by year. Again, you don't have to retain the categories these documents were in as Frequent Files; you can simply group them by year. As you work, set aside documents you want to place in your permanent archives. The rest goes into temporary archives, where they will be destroyed on a set future date.

For the most part, your financial archives will probably be of the temporary, not permanent, variety.

Choosing How Long to Archive

Be sure you're making an educated decision when you choose your destroy date. A professional organizer like myself can encourage you to keep only what you need, but we're not qualified to give you specific retention timelines. The IRS guideline for retaining tax-related documents used to be seven years, and many people are still comfortable with this timeframe (see the sidebar "How Long to Keep Records: What the IRS Says"), but if you're unsure, check with your accountant, insurance agent, or attorney.

Remember to give special attention to documents that belong in Safe Storage—items from any of the other groups that must be given extra protection from damage or theft. Examples of Safe Storage documents you might encounter while working with financial records include Social Security cards, birth or death certificates, and property deeds.

HOW LONG TO KEEP RECORDS: WHAT THE IRS SAYS

In a list of fear-based motivators, the IRS would rank at the top. Which would you prefer: A root canal with no anesthesia or a tax audit? Hmm, let me think about it.... Realistically, it's not that bad. If you don't cheat on your taxes and you have a system for saving papers that support items shown on your returns, you don't have much to worry about.

So, how long should you save those papers? The general IRS guideline used to be seven years, but it is now just three years, assuming you've been accurate in your reporting. During that time, you can amend your return to claim a refund and the IRS can, as they state it so diplomatically in Publication 552, "assess additional tax." That's three years from the period beginning after the return was filed, keeping in mind that returns filed before the due date are treated as being filed on the due date. You know what? I keep everything for four years just in case my definition of *year* is different from theirs.

If you've done anything dishonest, you do have reason for concern: There is no statute of limitations on IRS reviews of fraudulent returns or of people who didn't file a return and should have. If you underreported your income by more than 25%, they have six years instead of three to track you down.

Even if you've been a perfect angel, don't pitch it just because the IRS won't need it anymore. Your insurance or mortgage company might require even longer storage of some documents. When in doubt, check with your lender, insurance agent, or accountant.

To download the full text of "IRS Publication 552—Recordkeeping for Individuals," go to www.irs.gov and enter `Publication 552` in the Search Forms and Publications field.

Storing the Archived Documents

After you've completed this process, you'll have stacks of documents separated by year and designated for temporary archiving, a stack of documents for permanent archiving, and perhaps some items for Safe Storage. Move the Safe Storage items to a fire safe, safety deposit box at your bank, or another secure location. Some people also keep their permanent archive documents in a secure container or location.

You can store your Archives in any container that will keep them safe from water damage and pests. Plastic storage tubs are fine; just rubber band the year groupings and label them with their designated destroy date.

> **caution** Be careful not to let your archives become a repository of indecision! *Archives* should not be synonymous with *Stuff I Didn't Know What Else to Do With*. Make judicious choices—all your filing space, even in archives, is valuable and should not be cluttered with unneeded documents. Archives should also not be confused with memorabilia storage. Remember that the files we're talking about here are your financial records; storage of family photos and kids' artwork is a subject for another book.

Summary

Take a break and give yourself a reward: You've completed your Frequent Files, Archives, and Safe Storage projects! Up next: creating a set of Room by Room files to hold those warranties and instruction books that never seem to be handy when you need them. You'll also complete a major peace-of-mind project—an inventory of your belongings. Get ready to dive back into that trash can full of loose papers!

Proving It's Yours,
Or Should Be

One of the greatest advantages of getting your paperwork organized is that it enables you to quickly put your hands on any document during a crisis. Imagine tearing through file drawers, boxes, and piles, flinging everything onto the floor in a frantic search for your homeowner's insurance policy as the water in your basement rises. Not only would you waste precious time tracking down critical information, but you would also have a terrible mess to clean up later. Thankfully, now that you've completed Chapter 5, "Here to Stay: Storing Documents for Easy Retrieval," you've given yourself much better odds of finding what you need, when you need it; and, when you finish this chapter, your odds will be even better.

In the first part of this chapter, we'll do some more filing: This time, you will apply order to your warranties, instruction manuals, receipts, and other documents related to your belongings. This is the Room by Room project I promised you in Chapter 5.

You'll then use your Room by Room files to create a comprehensive inventory of your belongings. This is one of those projects that we all know we should do, but many of us never get around to it. When you've completed your inventory, you'll have one less thing to keep you awake at night. I recommend that you make both a text and a video inventory, and in this chapter I give you the steps to do both.

In this chapter:

* Build a set of files for papers related to your belongings
* Create a comprehensive property inventory

A comprehensive property inventory is an important step in protecting your finances. After you've completed your Room by Room files and property inventory, you will have a much better chance of collecting what you deserve if you need to make a claim on your homeowner's or renter's insurance. If there is any question as to exactly what you had or how much you paid for it, your records will help you establish the settlement amount that should be yours. Also, if ownership of any of your belongings is ever disputed, you'll know exactly where to go to produce documentation that it's yours.

Ready? Go back to that pile of loose papers you collected in Chapter 5 (at least it's smaller now, right?) and get ready to sort some more!

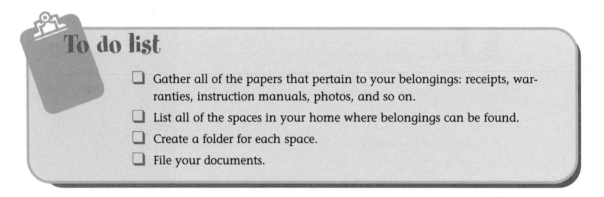

To do list

- ❑ Gather all of the papers that pertain to your belongings: receipts, warranties, instruction manuals, photos, and so on.
- ❑ List all of the spaces in your home where belongings can be found.
- ❑ Create a folder for each space.
- ❑ File your documents.

Building Your Room-by-Room Files

I've used this system myself for many years now, and most of my clients use it as well. It's one of my favorite organizing WOWs!

After years of maintaining three bulging, awkward files of warranties, instruction books, and receipts for all my belongings and still having trouble finding documentation when I needed it, I had an idea: Why not group all the information for an item together? It makes much more sense for the instruction manual, manufacturer's warranty, extended warranty, and receipt for the refrigerator to be kept all together, I reasoned. So I went through all of that paperwork and matched everything up by item.

The result? One humongous pile of information that was logically grouped on an individual level, but very inconvenient to access. My naturally categorical mind went to the next step: This single conglomeration needs some divisions. I tried making categories for the items, but soon became muddled with problems like how to decide whether the kitchen radio belonged with Small Appliances or Electronics. I needed a set of categories that would be indisputably clear.

Soon enough, a revelation struck: I might not remember whether I thought of an item as Small Appliances or Electronics, but I will certainly remember what room it's in—it's right there for me to see! My Room by Room system was born.

I made a folder for each room in my home and also for odd spaces like Hallway or Front Porch. I added Car, Purse, Work, and Self for things that I keep in my car, in my purse, at work, or on my person (such as a watch or glasses worn every day). Filing that huge pile of papers into my new Room by Room system was actually fun—and I hate filing. An example of this system is shown in Figure 6.1.

FIGURE 6.1

Here is a typical set of Room by Room files. This set employs sub-categories to group files according to whether the space is inside or outside the home and which floor it is on.

	Shed	
		In Van
		In Car
	Garage	
	Front Yard	
	Back Yard	
Outside		
		Bedroom-Ours
		Bedroom-Michael
		Bedroom-Bethany
	Upstairs	
		Living Room
		Kitchen
		Hall Closet
		Family Room
		Dining Room
		Bath-Main
		Bath-Half
	Main Floor	
		Storage Room
		Play Room
		Laundry
	Basement	
Inside		

Over time, the value of this system has become ever more obvious to me. Many times I've needed to grab a receipt, warranty, or instruction manual quickly—to tell an insurance agent or accountant how much I paid for something, check the date of purchase, or find the customer service phone number—and my Room by Room system has never failed me. I think you'll love it, too.

You'll need list

- ❑ Paper for making lists (or use your computer!)
- ❑ Hanging file folders
- ❑ Receipts, warranties, and instruction manuals for your belongings
- ❑ A table or desk for sorting

Gathering File Contents

Now that you have a plan for these types of documents, you can stop squirreling them away in kitchen drawers and garage cabinets. Instead, gather them all together for a glorious makeover. Pull out everything you'll need from that pile of loose papers you used to make your Frequent Files in Chapter 5 and collect other Room by Room items from kitchen drawers, your car, or other places you know they're lurking.

Over time, you'll find more of these documents around the house; just add them to your Room by Room system as you find them.

note You probably don't want or need to save every receipt for every little thing you buy, so consider setting a minimum cost or value and don't bother keeping receipts or warranties on items worth less than that amount. Continue adding these documents to your system as you find them—they tend to turn up in odd places.

Listing Your Spaces

Grab paper and pen and list all of the spaces where your belongings can be found. It might help to actually walk through your home and look for spaces you might not have thought of, such as hallways, foyers, or areas in your basement.

Include spaces that do not contain any belongings right now but that could in the future. For example, if there is currently nothing in your attic but you do intend to use it for storage eventually, include Attic on your list. (And congratulations on having an empty attic!) In contrast, if you have a crawl space under your home that is narrow, damp, and full of bugs, you probably won't ever store anything there, so don't list it.

Also list places outside your home that contain belongings of yours. This could include my previous examples (Car, Purse, Work, and Self), as well as Storage Unit, Mom's Basement, Dorm at School, or Safe Deposit Box.

Try to make your list as complete as possible, but don't worry if you miss a spot: You can always add it later.

When your list is done, you can start making files. Hold onto that list for the next section if you plan to use your computer for your belongings inventory.

Making Your Files

Grab a pen and your file folder tab inserts, and, just like you did in Chapter 5, write out your tabs. (Remember that a set of handwritten tabs is easier to add to than one based on label-making.) Create one folder for each space you've indicated on your list; if you find that you have more documents than will fit into one folder, you can add another behind the first.

Categorizing Room-by-Room Files

You have some opportunities for grouping and categorizing your Room by Room files. If you have what seems like a manageable number of files, you can forego categorizing and simply file the folders alphabetically. In this case, you might find it easier to group similar rooms together—for example all bedrooms, by naming them Bedroom—Ours, Bedroom—Kate's, and Bedroom—Guest instead of Our Bedroom, Kate's Bedroom, and Guest Room. This way, all the bedrooms are together under *B*, rather than one under *O*, one under *K*, and one under *G*. You can use the same principle for bathrooms and closets.

> **note** As you name your folders, remember to use the words that are natural to you. You might call the front room of your home the living room, whereas someone else would think of it as the sitting room. Use the names you've given to each of your spaces.

If you have a large number of spaces and therefore a large number of files, you might prefer to use some basic categories, such as those in Figure 6.1. You could begin by separating Inside files from Outside files, then subdivide the Inside files by floor, and finally alphabetize the files within each floor subset.

Some people like to go one step further and create subfolders for a category of items in a particular room. For example, you might like to have a folder for Toys as a subset of each child's bedroom folder.

If you employ categorization in your Room by Room files, remember to designate the hierarchy of your files with the appropriate tab position.

KEEP THE SYSTEM SIMPLE

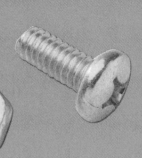

Don't go overboard and create an elaborate filing system that's more complex than it needs to be. Save yourself some time and frustration by making your Room by Room files only as detailed as absolutely necessary. If one folder for Outside will suffice, don't make separate Front Yard and Back Yard folders. For some folks, it's enough to have one folder named Bathrooms rather than one for each. Base your decision on how many items you have in each room and how big the folders will be if you keep the categories more general (a 5"-thick folder is probably not quite organized enough).

Filing Your Documents

Your folders are ready, and soon another large batch of wayward documents will be organized! At this point you have two options: The first option is to file everything you have in its appropriate room folder, regardless of how much it cost or even whether you're sure you still have the thing. This will get the paper out of your way for now and free you up to do something else; you can always come back later and weed out these files.

The other option is more precise and gives you greater functionality from the start, but of course it takes more work up-front. This option requires you to set some parameters regarding which documents to keep and which to toss.

Deciding What to Keep

If you tend to be a thorough person in thought and deed, this project could quickly become very time-consuming and tedious. I recommend that you resist the urge to keep absolutely everything and instead choose a method for identifying what should be kept and what can go straight to the trash.

The simplest criterion in this case is value. For each item for which you have a receipt plus a warranty or other documents, consider what the item cost and what it is worth now. Is it $5? $50? $500? At what dollar amount does saving the receipt with its accompanying documentation become not worth the effort?

Set a dollar amount to use as a general guideline, and keep receipts and ancillary documents only for items above that amount. There will be exceptions, of course: I kept the cardboard insert from the packaging on a really cool cat toy because I want to remember what it was and where to buy another when Bandit destroys the first one. I didn't keep the receipt, though; it cost only a few bucks, and it's not like I would claim it on my homeowner's policy if some other marauding feline absconded with it.

Consider the deductible amount on your property insurance policy when setting your dollar-amount guideline, but think twice before deciding to simply toss paperwork for any single item below that deductible amount. Remember that a loss often affects more than one item at a time, which could collectively add up to more than your deductible.

Filing It Away

With your keep-or-toss parameters in mind, weed out the documentation you don't need to save and file the rest. You will probably find paperwork on some things that you're not sure you still own; you can go ahead and file it for now or do a little investigating and clear up the mystery items. Eventually, as you maintain your system, you'll realize that you really do not still have that old vacuum or lamp, and you'll toss the paperwork.

You might also find paperwork on items you know are around somewhere, but are unsure about which room they're in. You can create a temporary folder in the front of your system to hold the paperwork for these homeless items until you track them down. Warning: The operative word here is *temporary*! If you dump everything into one big folder and label it Not Sure Which Room, you get an Incomplete on this project instead of an *A*.

Maintaining the System

Now that you have this fabulous new system for belongings paperwork, get into the habit of adding to it each time you purchase something with documents worth keeping. Say you buy a new TV. Staple the receipt to the owner's manual, tuck the warranty certificate inside, and file the whole thing in the folder for the room where the TV now resides. If you replaced another television in the process, pull out the paperwork for the old set and toss it, or, if you're giving the old TV away, give the recipients the paperwork along with the set.

Once in a while (say, once a year), go through your Room by Room files to weed out items you've gotten rid of and move paperwork for items that have been relocated to another area of your home.

And there you have it—relevant paperwork on all your belongings, handier than ever!

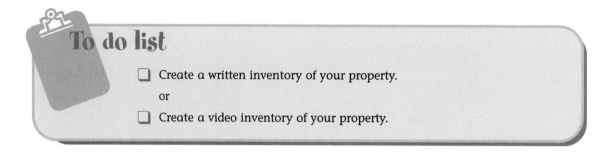

To do list

☐ Create a written inventory of your property.

or

☐ Create a video inventory of your property.

Creating a Property Inventory

Now for that peace-of-mind project: A property inventory.

You have several options with this project. You can create just the video inventory, just the paper or computer inventory, or both. Doing both is the most time-consuming but also the most comprehensive. If you choose this option, I recommend that you start with the video inventory and then watch it as you type your written list of possessions.

However you do it, if you end up with a complete inventory of your belongings, you'll be much better off than before!

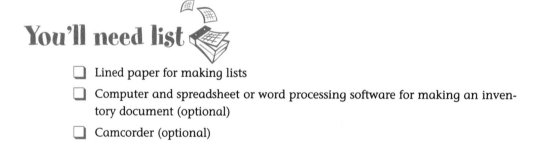

You'll need list

☐ Lined paper for making lists

☐ Computer and spreadsheet or word processing software for making an inventory document (optional)

☐ Camcorder (optional)

Taping It

A videotaped inventory of your belongings provides the all-important visual record that a written inventory cannot. However, it is not easy to search for a single item or to add to the video, so a written inventory is also important.

But, if you're going to complete just one piece of this project, let it be this one: It's far better than having nothing at all. Make a quick video, label it with the date, and store it away safely—ideally, in a fire safe rated for media or in a safe deposit box at the bank.

Use the camcorder to record all your belongings. Go room by room, narrating with a description of what is being seen on the tape (see the "Narrating Your Video" sidebar). Include whatever details come to mind, such as how you acquired the item, its age, or who owned it before you. Remember the basics such as the name of the item: For example, in my video, with the camera trained on a 3' rolling plastic contraption, I say, "This is the portable air conditioner in my office." You can add to these recollections in the supplemental paper inventory you will create in the section "Writing It."

What to Include

Some folks get lost in the details of creating a belongings inventory. In the interest of completeness, should you include every article of clothing, every item in your kitchen drawers, and every CD and DVD you own? If this could be your tendency, set some parameters before you begin.

Some people choose a minimum dollar value to qualify items for inclusion in their inventory, either video or paper (as you might have done when you created your Room by Room files previously). For example, I know that, realistically, if something I buy for less than $20 breaks after a few months, I'm not going to go to the trouble of returning it. I'll be displeased with the manufacturer, sure, and I won't buy that shoddy item again, but will I ever get around to taking it to the store and standing in line at the returns counter, or packaging it up and standing in line at the post office, all for $20? Probably not.

One caveat: Think twice before setting that dollar amount according to your property insurance deductible. If your deductible is $500 and you keep a record of only items worth more than that, you'll exclude most of your clothing, entertainment media, tools, and kitchenware. Categories like these are made up of many items that might be relatively inexpensive individually, but collectively they really add up. And if someone's going to steal from you, they won't take just one DVD—they'll take the whole shelf.

Figure out what your realistic dollar amount is: not your frugal ideal or the dollar amount your moral outrage will dictate (which for many of us is probably $1), but the amount that will actually motivate you to pursue compensation. Inventory only those items that meet or exceed your cutoff amount.

Here's another way to save time and keep your written inventory lean. Take a close-up view of a grouping of items of similar value (for example, a shot of all your books, close enough to read the title on each spine); then list just the count (for example, "75 paperbacks, 25 hardcovers") in your written inventory. You won't spend precious time recording every title in agonizing detail, yet if someone swipes a few handfuls of your DVDs, you'll be able to check your videotape to see which titles you lost.

NARRATING YOUR VIDEO

As you create your video inventory, take advantage of the opportunity to narrate with relevant details about the items you're recording. Mention anything you think might be meaningful, but try to at least include

* What the item is

* Where the item came from

* When you acquired it

* What it cost

Writing It

If you can find a way to bring your computer and your video into the same room, you'll have a great shortcut for creating your electronic inventory: Simply type in your inventory as you watch your video. If you have a laptop computer, you'll have no logistical problems. If you have only a desktop computer and your camcorder has a playback screen, you can watch the video on the camera itself while you type. If your camera does not have a playback screen, but you have a television and VCR in the vicinity of the computer, this option will still work for you.

If you have no way to watch your video as you type, you might find it more efficient to create your written inventory by hand rather than by computer, while watching your video in another room.

Synching Up Your Lists

No matter how you manage it, if you intend to create both a video and a written inventory, be sure that both match exactly. In other words, don't make the video and then go back through your rooms cataloging items without making sure you are capturing the same items and the information about them in both formats.

I used Microsoft Excel to create my belongings inventory (see Figure 6.2).

What to Include

Again, you can get bogged down if you attempt to include more detail than you need in your inventory. Begin with just the name of the item and where it is stored. For consistency with your video and with your Room by Room files, arrange the items in your written inventory by room. Beyond that, choose carefully what additional information you will commit yourself to gathering and maintaining.

FIGURE 6.2

Microsoft Excel is an excellent program for creating a property inventory database. Here is an example of a database with a separate worksheet for each room.

Item	Source	Acq. Date	Orig. Price/ Value	Replacemt Value (What ins. should pay)	Resale Value (eBay?)	Notes:
134 Maytag washer–model 432A	Sears	4/15/2000	$685.95	$750.00		
135 Maytag dryer–model 5634	Sears	4/15/2000	$850.00	$900.00		
136 Christmas tree	Target	12/2/1998	$99.99	$100.00	$25.00	
137 Recliner	Grammy & Grampy	6/12/1999	?	$300.00		Gift
138 Couch	Aunt Lil	6/12/1999	$1,499.00	$1,599.00	$500.00	Gift

After you've determined the details your insurance company would require of you in the event of a claim, add a column or line to your inventory for each category of information and fill in as many of these details as you can from the paperwork in your Room by Room files, your video, and your memory.

Maintaining It

A belongings inventory is never complete for long. No sooner will you finish this project than you or someone in your household will purchase something that needs to be added to the inventory.

You'll find it easier to make quick, ongoing additions to your written inventory than to your video. For this reason, I recommend that you get into the habit of updating your written inventory each time an item enters your life. Again, your parameters regarding what qualifies an item for inclusion will be helpful here. Your written inventory will soon become more up-to-date than your video, so once a year use your written inventory to narrate a new video.

tip I recommend that you contact the agent who handles your homeowner's or renter's insurance and ask exactly what information you would be required to provide to make a claim. Of course, the more information you have, the easier the claims process should be, but think hard before you commit yourself to keeping more details than you need. Ask your agent if and when details of manufacturer, production year, or seller are required. Ask whether you must state the item's purchase price and whether you would be required to produce a receipt to file a claim.

Summary

What a relief! You've got information, documents, and a videotape of everything you own, neatly organized. You've earned a nap, and I bet you'll sleep a bit more peacefully now.

What's more, you've reached the end of Part II, "Corral the Paper," and have completed all of the hard work of wrestling your financial papers into submission. Your financial documents, from incoming mail to pending bills to finance-related household files, are now sorted, purged, and easily accessible!

In the next chapter, I share some advanced organizing techniques—tricks that make my friends say, "We know you're organized; stop showing off!" Whether it's how I zip in and out of the grocery store, remember everything I've ordered online, and always know which DVDs I have, or the fact that I can buy Christmas supplies in July without duplicating what I already have, people tend to find my shopping efficiency awe-inspiring. Get ready to make your friends a little envious as well.

Part III

Advanced Projects

7   Be an Organized Consumer 111

8   Learn More from Your
     Organized Data 125

     Conclusion 139

A   Further Resources 143

Be an Organized Consumer

This chapter reminds me of the last week of classes each year in elementary school—those days when the academic work was done and we got to finish out the school year with puzzles, games, activities, and contests that let us put the year's new knowledge to use in fun ways.

You've studied hard and learned well in Chapters 1–6, so in this chapter you get to play. The projects you'll complete here will greatly enhance your efficiency as a consumer, which will in turn make shopping even more fun (if you already love it) or far less irritating (if, like me, you generally detest it). Once your friends and family catch on to what you're doing, you might just earn a reputation as the organized one!

Most important, as an organized shopper, you'll save money. When you shop with a list, know the store's layout, and visit only the aisles you need, you'll be less likely to make impulse purchases. When you're tracking your finances closely, you know exactly how much you have to spend and you're able to remain objective, making purchases that support your financial goals. When you maintain lists of the DVDs, CDs, or other collectibles you own, you prevent purchasing duplicates, and with running lists of gift ideas, you're always ready to buy the perfect birthday present without overspending due to indecision or desperation.

In this chapter, you complete several projects geared toward improving your shopping efficiency. We begin with a systematic approach to grocery shopping and

In this chapter:

- ✳ Organize your approach to grocery shopping to save time and money
- ✳ Clear out catalog clutter
- ✳ Learn to use lists to simplify shopping and reduce excess spending
- ✳ Track online/mail order purchase transactions

then attack the problem of catalog pile-up. We also create portable lists of categories of items like DVDs that leave you wondering, "Do I have this one?" Once-a-year shopping needs are also tough to remember, so we create another portable system for making the most of those "Christmas in July" sales. Finally, a method for capturing gift ideas so they're accessible when you're ready to buy and a tracking system for orders you've placed round out this chapter.

To do list

- [ ] Create a template to speed up grocery shopping.
- [ ] Replace paper catalogs with Web addresses.
- [ ] Create media lists for no-duplicate CD and DVD buying.
- [ ] Capture once-a-year shopping needs.
- [ ] Write wish lists for gift-giving and receiving.
- [ ] Set up a tracking system for orders placed.

No More Roaming the Aisles

In this section, you create maps of your frequently visited stores to use as shopping-list templates.

How many times have you gone to the grocery store for three specific things and left with a cartful? Do you ever get to use the 10 Items or Less lane?

Want to evolve from the accumulation that browsing produces into laser-guided, budget-friendly, super-efficient shopping? Great! Let's make a list!

Just kidding. We can do better than a plain old list. Instead, let's make a map (see Figure 7.1).

The next time you go grocery shopping, plan to spend some extra time there to begin this project. Take a large pad and pencil with you, and start at the service desk. Ask if they have a list of the items in each aisle or a map of the store. Use these items to inform the map you'll make, but don't rely on them completely: They're often out of date or not customized to the particular store you're in.

Sketch a rough diagram of where each section of the store is in relation to the other sections. For example, in Figure 7.1, the grocery aisles are on the left side of the store with dairy toward the back and the small appliances are found in the front right corner. This visual representation is better than a simple list because it reminds me that if I need ice cream and batteries, I'd better start with the batteries because the ice cream will melt by the time I trek all the way over to the batteries!

FIGURE 7.1

Take your grocery list to new heights: Combine your shopping list with a map of the store and you'll be in and out in no time, with less impulse-buying and no forgotten items. This illustration is a map of my local Meijer store with commonly purchased items preprinted so I can just circle them as needed.

11: Dairy/Milk/Paper: Milk Eggs TP Paper towels Yogurt	Bottle Return?	Paint, Plumbing, Elec., Hardware
	Health & Beauty: Ibuprofen Toothpaste Shampoo Conditioner Razors Deodorant	
Cheese, Frozen Rolls/Cookies: Cheese slices		
10: Paper, Picnic, Laundry: Laundry soap Ziplocs—Gal, Quart, Sand Paper plates Kleenex		
9: Laundry, Cleaning, Pets: Bleach Softener Cascade Jet Dry Liq. Soap Cat food Litter Light bulbs	Cosmetics/Hair Access:	
8: Baking, Spices: Peppercorns	Auto, Sports, Furniture:	
7: Bulk, Coffee, Drink Mixes: Coffee Cocoa Creamer	Cards, Books, Party, Home Fashions, Housewares: Brita Filters	Seasonal, Shelving:
6: Bulk Frozen/Canned		
Meat: Hamburger Chicken Pork chops		Toys:
5: Juice, Canned Fruit/Vegs, Pkg. Dinners, Potatoes/Rice: Fruit cups Apple juice Mac & cheese		
4: Tuna, Sauces, Condiments, Mexican/Chinese: Tuna lunch kits	Clothes, Shoes:	Gifts, Lamps, Candles
3: PB & J, Soup, Cereal/Breakfast: Peanut butter Tomato soup Cereal Fruit & Grain bars		
2: Chips, Pop: Baked Lay's		Pets, Garden
1: Bread, Cookies, Crackers: Bread Graham crackers		
Alcoholic Bevs, Crackers, Party Cheese/Deli: Popcorn Nuts Saltines		
Frozen: Lean Cuisines		Jewelry/Photo/Sm. Appliance: Batteries
Produce: Apples Bananas Grapes Tomatoes Salad Peppers		
Deli, Bakery: Sliced turkey Sliced ham		

Now fill in the details. With a store like the one in Figure 7.1, you'll probably find that you need more detail in the grocery aisles and can stop with the general section description in the other areas. Walk the grocery aisles and write down the locations of your most commonly purchased items. When you go home, you'll type or write these common items into your map so you can circle them as you run out.

For example, in aisle 8, the only thing I buy frequently is whole peppercorns, so I've listed them for easy circling. If I happen to need an unusual spice or if I want to bake a cake (rare!), I write in the ingredients I need.

When you've completed your sketch and item locations, go ahead and do your shopping. Then head home to your desk. Use the Tables function in Microsoft Word to create a one-page map of the store and type in your commonly purchased items in their aisles or sections. If you prefer, you can use a ruler to redraw your draft sketch. When you're satisfied with your map, make copies and post one where it will be convenient to add to, such as your kitchen bulletin board or inside the pantry door.

You'll need list

- ❑ Your computer and spreadsheet software
- ❑ Your planner
- ❑ Paper and pencil

Whenever you run out of an item, circle or write it on your store map. Now when you go grocery shopping, you'll be done in record time and will have purchased only what you need. And, of course, remember to record that transaction in your financial management system!

Some people use more than one grocery store, and some have an additional produce market or warehouse club they frequent. If this is true of you, create maps for each so you can enjoy the same organized efficiency everywhere you shop.

Reducing Bulky Catalog Clutter

In this section, you replace your paper catalog collection with a weightless, clutter-free, online shopping system.

If you sometimes shop by mail order rather than in an actual store, you probably have lots of catalogs lying around. You might even have a system for organizing those catalogs. Kind of cumbersome, huh? Let's make this process easier.

A client of mine named Allison had a large file drawer of alphabetized catalogs, and she struggled to keep up with the task of replacing old ones with the new editions that flooded her mailbox every day. She was committed to making the system work for a number of reasons: She appreciates the time savings of shopping from home; she knows she is more likely to make impulse purchases when handling merchandise in an actual store; and, in building her catalog collection, she had learned which companies offer the best prices, best service, and highest-quality merchandise.

So, for Allison, catalog shopping makes excellent financial sense. However, as her life became ever more busy, she found herself falling further behind in maintaining her system and the catalogs started to pile up.

We used the Internet to upgrade Allison's system. She had been keeping her catalogs for many years, before the companies also had an online shopping option, as most do now. What a relief it was when Allison realized she could keep a list of her catalog Web sites and toss the paper copies!

I knew Allison would resist the idea of simply pitching all her catalogs, even though more would eventually come in the mail, because she was keeping the paper copies for two reasons: to be able to see the products the companies offer and to remember that those particular companies exist. For her, the key to making an educated buying decision is to have an entire virtual mall at her fingertips, not to be limited to settling for whatever she can find in whatever catalog happens to be on the coffee table. I also knew she would not be satisfied with simply adding each Web site to the Favorites list in her browser because she wanted a way to include notes and to categorize what each company offers.

We created a spreadsheet in Microsoft Excel (like the one in Figure 7.2) and Allison used her accumulated catalogs to list the name and Web site of each. Next to these columns she added some categories for things she shops for frequently, such as clothing and gifts, and checked off the appropriate categories for each catalog. Finally, and with great satisfaction, she tossed the paper catalogs.

Occasionally, Allison found a catalog from a company that did not have an online store; she kept the paper catalogs for some of these and decided the others weren't that important anyway and could be tossed. Now, instead of an entire drawer of catalogs and the daily task of replacing old copies with new ones, Allison has a comprehensive Excel list that tells her at a glance which companies are best for any category, meaning comparison shopping has never been easier.

FIGURE 7.2
Dump the pounds of paper and create a list of your favorite catalogs' Web sites instead.

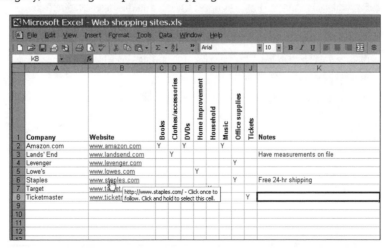

Allison has also gotten into the habit of telling companies that she no longer wants paper catalogs by checking order form boxes that let her opt out of mailings or telling the phone operator to take her off the mailing list. The number of new catalogs arriving each day is gradually dwindling, but the opt-out procedure is different with each company, so it's tedious. Until the law changes and consumers have to take special steps to opt *in* to receiving catalogs, Allison and the rest of us will probably never be able to escape them completely.

Want to lose the catalog collection and switch to an electronic list? Go for it! Use Figure 7.2 as a sample and draw up your own list. Then scour your home for paper catalogs, enter their Web addresses into your list, and toss them!

You can create your list easily on paper, but if you do it in Excel you'll gain two additional functions: You'll be able to sort by category (so, for example, when you want to buy clothes, you can group together all of the sites where you shop for clothing), and you'll be able to set the Web addresses as hyperlinks that will open the site in your browser with a click from within the Excel sheet. This is better than simply adding them to your browser's Favorites list because you can add your own notes, such as item numbers and ideas for future purchases.

note To pare down the junk invading your mailbox, see "Take Me Off Your List!" in Chapter 4, "Fighting the Data Deluge."

IS YOUR BUYING TOO IMPULSIVE?

If you're trying to curb your spending, notice which types of shopping are hardest for you to control. Some people are able to remain objective when shopping by mail order, but in a store, once they literally get their hands on something, they simply must buy it. For others, shopping in person is relatively controllable but a paper catalog in hand or an image on a Web site is too much of a temptation. If shopping in person triggers overspending, keep control with the Web-based system in this chapter. If paper catalogs are too enticing, make an extra effort to remove yourself from mailing lists, and if Web sites encourage you to overspend, perhaps it would be better not to keep a list of them. Knowing which shopping style provokes an overly impulsive response can help you avoid it.

If you find you just can't stop spending, whether in person or by mail order, consider talking to a therapist who can help you discover the reason and work toward a solution. Visit www.stoppingovershopping.com for more information.

Becoming a Master Listmaker for More Organized Shopping

In this section, you set up lists to carry in your paper planner or PDA that will maximize gift-giving, collection-building, and holiday/seasonal supply purchases. Keeping lists of these items contributes to your financial organization in several ways: It helps you to budget for future purchases, allows you to plan purchases calmly rather than making them as a knee-jerk reaction in the store, and prevents duplication or overbuying because you've forgotten what you already have.

How many times have you been in a store, discovered something you need or want—on sale!—and wished you had the specifics so you'd know what size, color, or model to buy? Now you'll never have to wonder: You can carry that information with you wherever you go.

This is the biggest advantage of a PDA over a paper planner: the sheer volume of data you can conveniently carry with you. I utilize the Notes section of my PDA to the absolute max, with dozens of lists including the ones in this chapter. When a sale sneaks up on me, I'm always ready.

Don't have a PDA? You can still take advantage of this improvement. Just make your lists on paper to keep in your planner, or, if you don't carry your paper planner with you when you go shopping (and many people don't), just type up your lists in your computer's word processing program, make the font and type size as small as you can read, print them, and cut them into wallet-size pieces. Save the file on the computer and update it as needed.

Listing Things You Need and Things You Already Have

DVDs seem to be the only type of media that I need to keep in list form. I've found that it's not so hard to remember whether I have a particular CD, but because we can either rent or buy movies and video games, if it's one I've already seen, it's hard to recall whether it was borrowed or purchased when it last graced my TV screen.

So, one of the lists in my PDA is of DVDs I own (see Figure 7.3 for an example). I also keep a list of DVDs I want to buy and another list of movies I want to rent. (Yep, I rely on my memory for very little!)

Why not make your own list right now? Even if you can't find all of your movies in one search, at least start your list: A partial record is better than none. If you think you own a movie but can't find it, list it with a question mark.

If you decorate your home for various holidays, you might have already thought of another application for this idea.

FIGURE 7.3

Here's an example of a list of DVDs to carry with you to prevent duplication when adding to your collection.

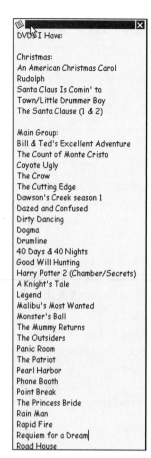

```
DVDs I Have:

Christmas:
An American Christmas Carol
Rudolph
Santa Claus Is Comin' to
Town/Little Drummer Boy
The Santa Clause (1 & 2)

Main Group:
Bill & Ted's Excellent Adventure
The Count of Monte Cristo
Coyote Ugly
The Crow
The Cutting Edge
Dawson's Creek season 1
Dazed and Confused
Dirty Dancing
Dogma
Drumline
40 Days & 40 Nights
Good Will Hunting
Harry Potter 2 (Chamber/Secrets)
A Knight's Tale
Legend
Malibu's Most Wanted
Monster's Ball
The Mummy Returns
The Outsiders
Panic Room
The Patriot
Pearl Harbor
Phone Booth
Point Break
The Princess Bride
Rain Man
Rapid Fire
Requiem for a Dream
Road House
```

I decorate inside for Christmas and I make a spooky yard display for Halloween, so I keep lists in my PDA for each of these holidays (see Figure 7.4). Updating the list is part of the preparation and disassembly chores each year: As I wrap gifts for Christmas, I note whether I'm running out of tissue paper or boxes; as I disassemble the cardboard coffin and tombstones on November 1, I update my Halloween list so I'll remember to get more fog machine solution next year.

The system paid off last summer when I found an entire aisle of pre-pre-PRE-Christmas loot on sale at our local warehouse club. I checked my PDA, found that I needed tissue paper but still had tons of gift bags, and was able to take advantage of this unexpected opportunity, getting exactly what I needed and nothing that I didn't.

FIGURE 7.4

Make lists of once-a-year supplies while they're on your mind at the time of the holiday. Rely on your memory months later and you'll end up with 25 rolls of wrapping paper and no gift boxes, or two coffins and no Dracula.

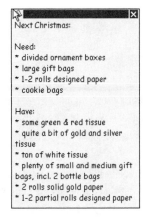

Next Christmas:

Need:
* divided ornament boxes
* large gift bags
* 1-2 rolls designed paper
* cookie bags

Have:
* some green & red tissue
* quite a bit of gold and silver tissue
* ton of white tissue
* plenty of small and medium gift bags, incl. 2 bottle bags
* 2 rolls solid gold paper
* 1-2 partial rolls designed paper

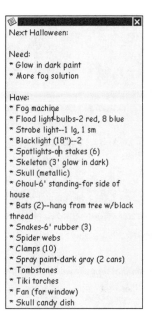

Next Halloween:

Need:
* Glow in dark paint
* More fog solution

Have:
* Fog machine
* Flood light-bulbs-2 red, 8 blue
* Strobe light--1 lg, 1 sm
* Blacklight (18")--2
* Spotlights-oh stakes (6)
* Skeleton (3' glow in dark)
* Skull (metallic)
* Ghoul-6' standing-for side of house
* Bats (2)--hang from tree w/black thread
* Snakes-6' rubber (3)
* Spider webs
* Clamps (10)
* Spray paint-dark gray (2 cans)
* Tombstones
* Tiki torches
* Fan (for window)
* Skull candy dish

Who Wants What: Maintaining Gift Lists

Which is better: Wandering the mall for gift-giving inspiration or dashing in and grabbing exactly what people want? You can be the perpetual giver of the perfect gift (and always know what to request for yourself as well) with the lists you create in this section. These are lists that are never complete and never go away; you just keep adding to them and deleting from them.

What They Want

Let's start by making one list called Gift Ideas—Others. As you did for your DVDs a minute ago, make a simple Word document, PDA note, or handwritten list and include everything you can think of that would appeal to the lucky recipients in your life. Also include sizes, brands, prices, and stores where specific items are sold.

After you collect all of this information, you might not need to look at it until months later, and it's at that point that you'll realize what a good idea this list is because you will have forgotten some of the ideas captured here!

Your Gift Ideas—Others list is a great alternative to shopping year-round and packing your closets with gifts to be given later. That habit solves one organizational problem—do it while you're thinking of it—but creates another: compromised storage space. Adding to your list as inspiration strikes takes advantage of your do-it-now habit without filling up valuable space (and you won't have to dust those gifts before you wrap them).

ANOTHER WAY TO CURB IMPULSE-BUYING

One of the characteristics of attention deficit disorder is impulsivity, and because many of my clients have ADD, we're always looking for ways to satisfy an impulse without getting off-track organizationally. Lists like the ones you create in this section are a big help if you tend to buy impulsively.

People often buy things not because they have no discipline and can't deny themselves anything but because, if they don't buy it right then, they'll forget about it. Seeing the item either gives you the idea that you want it or reminds you that you wanted it in the past but forgot about it. That awareness, which you know will last just moments, provokes a strong feeling of urgency toward acquiring that item immediately.

You can satisfy that urgency without spending a penny simply by adding the item to your list. Now you've acquired the idea or memory, and you can get the actual item later.

What I Want

Okay, you have Gift Ideas—Others. Now make Gift Ideas—Me! People say I'm silly to suggest you would need to make a list to remember everything *you* want, but think about it: If someone wanted to know, right now, five things you would like for your birthday, you'd have to give it some thought, wouldn't you?

I'm not talking about the convertible Saleen Mustang—the fantasy stuff is always easy to remember (and, sigh, not likely to materialize). I'm talking about the smaller things you encounter day by day and you think, "Hmm, that would be nice to have," but then as Mother's Day approaches, you can't think of a thing you need, so in desperation they get you another lace-collared sweatshirt.

Start writing down those kinda-neat things you admire as you're shopping for someone else, flipping through a catalog, or watching TV. Include titles of movies you'd like to own on video or DVD, CDs of that band with the nice harmonies that you saw on *The Tonight Show*, clever gadgets and pretty candles from your friends' home-sale parties…anything you see that strikes your fancy but for whatever reason doesn't get purchased on the spot.

By the way, if any of my gift givers are interested, I'd love a Detroit Red Wings jersey with my own last name on it. (Stanley, get it? Hockey? Stanley Cup? Cute, huh?) And the only reason I can remember that right this moment is because it's on my Gift Ideas—Me! list.

What the House Needs

Depending on how needy your home is, you can make a simple, uncategorized list like the one in Figure 7.5, or you can group items by room, by store, or by price. Thankfully, my list has gotten fairly short, but two years ago when I'd just purchased my house, there were at least five items for every room!

My list now includes items to replace occasionally, such as the furnace filter and odd-sized light bulbs. I note the brand I prefer, the model number, the size, the store that had the item for the best price the last time I bought it, and what that price was.

Some household purchases are so infrequent that they're easy to forget to include in a budget; a list like this not only helps you make a more comprehensive budget, but also gives you an idea of how much the budget amount should be—something you're not likely to remember if it's not recorded.

Get into the habit of adding items to your list whenever you acquire something with a part that will eventually need to be replaced. For example, if you buy a new halogen desk lamp, add the bulb size and model number to your list. Then, when the bulb burns out, you'll be ready to purchase the right replacement bulb on the first try.

FIGURE 7.5

A list like this, carried in your wallet, planner, or PDA, means you're always ready to buy what you need for your home. Carry similar lists of gift ideas for others— and for yourself!

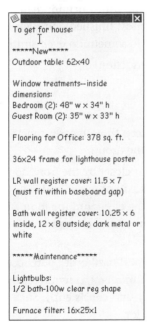

```
To get for house:
    I
*****New*****
Outdoor table: 62x40

Window treatments--inside
dimensions:
Bedroom (2): 48" w × 34" h
Guest Room (2): 35" w × 33" h

Flooring for Office: 378 sq. ft.

36x24 frame for lighthouse poster

LR wall register cover: 11.5 × 7
(must fit within baseboard gap)

Bath wall register cover: 10.25 × 6
inside, 12 × 8 outside; dark metal or
white

*****Maintenance*****

Lightbulbs:
1/2 bath-100w clear reg shape

Furnace filter: 16x25x1
```

For optimum efficiency and savings, your list should include measurements, colors, brands, model numbers, prices, and any other data that will allow you to buy without first running home to get more information. I'd much rather walk up to the plumbing guy at Lowe's and ask him to order me "the American Standard Cadet pedestal sink in white, model #0236.811 with three faucet holes, not just one," rather than ask him to help me find "a sink to match a toilet that kind of looks like that one over there...."

With this approach, a woman can talk to almost any hardware store clerk without having to hear that infuriating line, "Why don't you just send your husband in?" Considering what I would say in response, avoiding that conversation actually spares the clerk's pride more than my own.

Never Again Wonder, "Did I Get That?"

Okay, you have lists, you have a database—you're a super-efficient shopper! You've placed orders all over the Internet and now you can kick back and wait for your stuff to come to your door! And a week from now, you'll forget you ordered it and they can just keep your money!

Hey, wait a minute....

There's one more step to add to each mail-order transaction: the follow-through. You can make another list, but this chapter's almost finished and even I am sick of list-making by now, so I bet you are, too. Let's do something even simpler:

1. Print or write some record of the transaction.
2. Post it with other transaction records.

This is one of those beautiful systems that is just so elegant in its simplicity. All you have to do is record each transaction and keep those records together somewhere. When an item arrives, pull its record from the group.

I like to use a clipboard hung inside my coat closet by the front door. I just print the order confirmation or scribble a note on a scrap of paper and stick it in the clipboard. If an item seems to be lingering on the clipboard too long, I'm prompted to open QuickBooks and see whether the payment has cleared or call the company and check the item's status.

Use whatever works for you to track online and mail-order purchases. Use sticky notes on the fridge, a message board by the mailbox, a reminder in your planner—anything, as long as you'll use it completely and consistently. Such a method ensures that you always get what you paid for.

Ah, one more contribution to your peace of mind!

Summary

Did you ever think shopping could be so organized? Go ahead, gloat: You have systems to be proud of! You can walk into any store or browse any Web site and know what you need and what you don't, what's a great idea, and what's a passing whim. You can run that grocery store like a sprint or like a marathon because you're in control, and you'll never again find yourself out of fake blood on Halloween. If sticking to a budget is a priority for you, you'll find it's now much easier to do because with all your options listed objectively, you can easily see which purchases are most important and which can wait.

Just one more chapter and you'll be done with your financial organization overhaul. In that final chapter, you get an introduction to some advanced tools for analyzing your newly organized data—a taste of what you might want to investigate next, on your own or with the help of your accountant, investment broker, or other financial advisor. Let's go crunch some numbers!

Learn More from Your
Organized Data

N ow that you have your numbers in order, what do you want to do with them? Perhaps your goal in working through this book was to get your financial data organized so you can make an accurate budget or decide how best to divide your income among expenses and investments. Maybe you're deep in debt and need a plan for getting out of it, or you have a big expense coming up and want to start saving now. Those are all excellent goals, and they're an example of the point at which a professional organizer would refer you to an accountant, broker, or other financial expert for specialized advice on saving, investing, and managing your money.

In this chapter, we touch on each of these projects to give you some ideas for investigating further on your own or with a financial advisor.

In this chapter:

* Calculating your personal profits and losses
* Assessing your debt
* Taking a close look at your spending patterns
* Measuring your debt-to-income ratio
* Using your organized data to help manage your budget

To do list

- ❑ Calculate your net worth.
- ❑ Calculate your debt-to-income ratio.
- ❑ Create a personal profit-and-loss statement.
- ❑ Make a detailed record of your debt.
- ❑ Analyze your spending patterns.
- ❑ Create a budget.

Calculating Your Personal Profits and Losses

Let's get this chapter off to a strong start by looking at you as not just one person but as a serious, complex financial operation. As such, you need to periodically assess your financial health. The standard measurement of financial health for a business is the profit and loss statement (P&L). This is a simple calculation of how much money the company made, minus expenses, which shows what the net profit or loss was for a given time period (for example, one fiscal year).

You'll need list

- ❑ Your income and expense tracking document from Chapter 1
- ❑ Your bill-paying system, medical bill tracking document, and "Did I Pay That?" record from Chapter 3
- ❑ The files you created in Chapters 5 and 6
- ❑ Any other information relevant to your financial status

It might seem strange to think of yourself as a business and to look at your income and expenses in terms of profit and losses to that business. Yet that oddness is precisely what makes this and the following exercises so useful. If you've never arranged your financial data in this way, doing so will give you a fresh perspective and provide insights you might never have divined solely from your checkbook and bank statement.

People generally don't have fiscal years—we just have years. And we don't think of our lives as having a profit or a loss—we either made good money last year or we didn't. Most of us don't start the new year by calculating how our fourth-quarter figures affected the bottom line in the annual report: We're just trudging through the winter months and dreading the credit card bills from the holidays. But looking at your personal life from this businesslike perspective can be enlightening, so let's do it.

Using the tools you created in the earlier chapters of this book, choose the system that contains your most complete income and expenditure information for the year. This might be your income and expense tracking document from Chapter 1, "Tracking Your Money," or it could be the bill-paying system you created in Chapter 4, "Fighting the Data Deluge." If you've been moving money into a savings account (and you haven't spent it), be careful *not* to include those funds in your expenses.

note Your tax accountant might not be able to work directly with you to create a budget, but she can probably suggest a good book or another consultant who can help you. Look under Financial Services or Credit and Debt Counseling Services in your local telephone directory for more names. Debt counselors are experts at making budgets, and you don't have to wait until you're in serious debt to seek their assistance. There are also many useful Web sites and software packages available to inform your financial decision-making (see the Further Resources that follow this chapter).

If you've entered all of your financial data into a money-management software program like Quicken or Microsoft Money, you'll find the totals you need within the program. You'll probably even find a report within the program that will make this calculation for you; just take care to set up the report correctly so it will use data from all of your accounts and give you an accurate result. Until you're very confident with this software, it might be best to make these calculations by hand, at least as a way to check the program's results.

Using Figure 8.1, start with the most basic version of a P&L calculation.

FIGURE 8.1

This is a profit-and-loss statement at its most basic. Fill in your income and expenditures for the year. If income is higher, you made a profit; if not, you took a loss.

Total Income for Year 20__	$
Total Expenditures for Year	-$
Difference	$

Now you have one number—the difference between your income and your expenditures—and it's either your profit or your loss for the year.

Big deal, you're thinking, what does that really tell me? As it stands, this number doesn't tell you much. You need more detail to understand how that single number came to be so it can be either corrected or replicated in the future.

You can flesh out both the income and the expense portions of the P&L to better analyze why that bottom line ended up the way it did. Try subcategorizing the expense section using the categories you set up in your income and expense tracking document and your bill-paying system. Subtotal each category and brace yourself: You might be shocked to see what groceries add up to over an entire year.

You can also add detail to the income section of the P&L. Do you have more than one source of income, and if so, which was the most profitable?

If your P&L shows less profit than you want, use the rest of the tools in this chapter to pinpoint the problem and do something about it.

Getting In-Depth with Your Debt

When the P&L shows a loss, you have two choices: find more income or reduce expenses. Unfortunately, both can be tough to do. Some expenses, such as loans, are obligations that you can't just stop paying (see Figure 8.2).

FIGURE 8.2

Use a chart like this to recategorize your expenses and see them in a new light. If you have a lot of installment-loan payments in the third column, check out Figure 8.3 for a way to keep closer track of them.

Could Stop	Might Be Reducible	Stuck With It
Magazine subscriptions	Electric bill	Mortgage
	Phone bill	Visa balance
		Car payment
		Tuition

Take a fresh look at your overall expenses by separating the things you can reduce (utility bills) or stop (subscriptions, lattes, and so on) from the things you're stuck with (installment loans such as a mortgage, revolving loans such as credit card debt, and the like). Create a table like the one in Figure 8.2 and fill in all of your expenditures. If you find that you have several loans in the "Stuck with It" category, creating a more detailed view of those items will help you to anticipate when you'll be done paying on them; this is critical information if you plan to create a budget later in this chapter.

To give yourself a better vantage point on your loan debt, create a chart or table similar to the one in Figure 8.3. If you've never done this before, make sure you're sitting down: Seeing your debt totaled this way can be a real shocker.

FIGURE 8.3

A chart listing all of your installment- and revolving-loan debt, including interest rates and time frames, is a useful first step toward deciding how best to pay it all off.

Liability (in payoff priority order; pay highest int rates 1st)	Amt Owed ...	Credit Limit	Int. Rate	Min. Pymt	... As Of	Notes
Citibank MC	8,751.21	8,460.00	27.990	210.00	1/20/04	Took $2000 cash advance to pay Ron for flood; higher int rate on adv
Amex	5,424.84	5,000.00	23.990	300.00	1/8/04	Was originally 14.99%--???
MBNA Visa	1,973.75	2,500.00	12.990	50.00	1/23/04	
MBNA WorldPoints Visa	10,240.14	10,000.00	9.900	200.00	1/12/04	Started 3/25/03 @ $8228.03--transferred Citibank to here; 5/03, add
Bank--overdraft protection	356.02	1,000.00	9.900	70.00	3/31/04	7/30/03: Not getting bills, address still not changed, sent fax
Total Credit Debt	**26,745.96**					
Mortgage	135,081.31		7.250		12/30/03	30-yr loan; started 8/13/02 @ $136,800
2nd Mortgage	34,019.70		11.375		12/30/03	15-yr loan; started 8/13/02 @ $34,200 and 11.655% int.
Total Mortgage Debt	**169,101.01**					
TOTAL LIABILITIES	**195,846.97**					

When you see what you're facing, you can plan your attack. (This is a great time to consult a financial advisor.) Strategize the best way to knock down your debt (for example, in Figure 8.3, you might notice this person has chosen to pay off items with the highest interest rates first) and keep yourself on track by updating this chart every month.

WHAT TO DO WHEN DEBT IS TOO DEEP

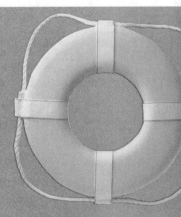

What do you do when your debt has become truly unmanageable? If, despite your best efforts, organizing your finances and creating a budget just aren't going to be enough, you might need to consider a more drastic measure, such as declaring bankruptcy. Information on how to file for bankruptcy is available at www.uscourts.gov/bankruptcycourts.html.

If you suspect (or know) that you would have enough money if you could just stop spending it, you might find relief with Debtors Anonymous (www.debtorsanonymous.org). This organization employs the 12-step approach popularized by Alcoholics Anonymous to help people learn to control their spending. The Web site features a quiz to determine whether you are a compulsive debtor and some resources for suggested reading.

Taking a Close Look at Your Spending Patterns

Now that you have a new perspective on your installment- and revolving-loan debt and have identified your expenses as either reducible or not, look at your expenditures once more and try to spot patterns. Sort them every which way—by month, by year, by store, by category. (Yes, this is much easier if you're using software.)

For example, is the total you spent on gifts higher than you wish, even though each item seemed to be of a manageable price at the time you bought it? This is information that might help you keep a big-picture perspective when shopping for an acquaintance's bridal gift. Do you still love all of the shoes you bought last year enough to justify their prices? If so, you're validated; if not, you'll now find shopping at discount stores even more appealing.

tip As I've said before, don't let guilt get in the way of your progress here. If you're dismayed to see what you spent last year or last month, don't dwell on the past: Use that information to make positive changes going forward. Now that you can see all of last year's decisions together at one time and compare them to one another, you finally have the information you need to make your best choices—information you didn't have before, so it's no wonder you couldn't make those best choices in the past. Now you can!

PUT A PRICE ON YOUR HEAD

The other calculations in this chapter focus on your cash flow, which can be pretty depressing at times. If you own a home, a car, or anything else that's worth money, here's a formula that might make you feel a little better: Your net worth.

Cash isn't the whole story; other assets count, too.

To do this accurately, you need to know what your assets are worth: all of your investments, plus the market value of your house, vehicle(s), jewelry, art, and so on. You also need an up-to-date reckoning of your liabilities (refer to Figure 8.3).

Total the money in each of your accounts and the value of everything you own; then subtract your liabilities. The resulting figure is your net worth.

For excellent step-by-step instructions for net worth and many other useful calculations, visit the AARP Web site (`www.aarp.org/financial`).

Do You Live Beyond Your Means?

That's a loaded question, and a tricky one, too, because there are many opinions regarding exactly what "your means" are. When the question is being asked by a lender considering granting you a mortgage, lease, or credit card, he or she will answer it at least partially by calculating your debt-to-income ratio.

Basically, this calculation tells a lender how much money you'll have left to pay his or her loan after you've paid for everything you're already committed to. It would be impossible to catalog here all of the methods lenders use for determining your debt-to-income ratio: The very definition of what constitutes income and debt varies from lender to lender.

For the purpose of organizing your finances, these definitions are quite simple: *Income* is any money you can expect to receive on a regular basis (for example, your take-home pay and child support or alimony payments you receive if they arrive reliably), and *debt* is anything you are committed to paying (installment loans such as a mortgage, revolving loans such as credit card payments, and child support or alimony that you pay; refer to the items you listed in Figure 8.3). Debt does not include expenses such as utilities or groceries; these are living expenses—not loans. Add up your monthly debt payments, divide by your monthly net income, and you have your debt-to-income ratio.

Figure 8.4 shows the simplest way to calculate your debt-to-income ratio, which tells you how much of a financial safety net you currently have. Keep in mind that this figure is useful for your information, but it probably won't match what a lender would calculate if you applied for a loan.

FIGURE 8.4

Using your income and loan expenses for an average month, calculate your debt-to-income ratio. Under 10% is considered excellent, 10%–20% is okay, and over 20% could be risky.

	You	Example
Total debt payments for month (e.g., mortgage, car loan, credit cards, child support, or alimony you pay)	$	$1200
Divided by	÷	÷
Total income for month (e.g., your take-home pay, child support, or alimony you receive)	$	$4500
Overall debt-to-income ratio	%	26.7%

Experts tend to agree that you can breathe easy with a debt-to-income ratio below 10% and that you're still fairly safe up to 20%. Knowing your debt-to-income ratio can help you to make prudent choices when you're in the market for a new home or vehicle. Having already calculated this ratio *your* way, you can make a more informed choice if a lender uses her own method of calculating your debt-to-income ratio and offers you more money than you know you can afford. Remember, lenders often allow you to take on more debt than you should. It's up to you to set prudent limits for yourself.

caution If your debt-to-income ratio is above 20%, you're on thin ice because your available incoming funds wouldn't be enough to carry you through an emergency without incurring more debt. If your debt-to-income ratio is high and suddenly the dog needs surgery or the furnace dies, you'll most likely have to take a loan to pay for it. Oh, the irony. This must be why they say having debt just leads to more debt.

HOW MUCH HOUSE PAYMENT CAN YOU AFFORD?

As I've said, I'm no financial expert, but here's one thing I do know: Many lenders are happy to give you enough financial rope to hang yourself, especially for a mortgage. If you default on the loan, they'll just take the house back, keep the money you paid, and start fresh with a new borrower. It's up to you to stay within your means and only borrow what *you* know you can afford, which might not be the entire amount they're willing to give you.

"But my lender seems so knowledgeable," you might say. "He showed me a formula based on my income that proves I can afford the house I want." Some lenders use the 28/36 qualifying ratio to calculate how much to lend you. The numbers are percentages of your gross income: either 28% or 36% of what you earn before taxes or any other deductions. Lenders following this ratio will allow you to commit a maximum of 28% of your gross income for housing expenses or a maximum of 36% of that gross for housing expenses plus your other recurring debt. However, there is variation among lenders in what constitutes housing expenses and recurring debt and also in how strictly this ratio is applied. Furthermore, some lenders use a different calculation altogether. And, just to make it more confusing, a budget counselor is likely to give you a very different opinion: Many will suggest that you calculate what you can afford based on your net—not your gross—income and their allowable percentages will be more conservative.

The critical fact to keep in mind when deciding how much to borrow is this: Just because a lender will give it to you doesn't mean it's a good idea. You—not the lender—are the only one who can decide what's in your best interests.

Using Your Data to Organize a Budget

By now, all of this microscopic examination of your financial data might have inspired you to create a budget. We're getting very close to the point where I, the professional organizer, wish you well and hand you over to your financial advisor. But, in the spirit of organizing your data without judging it, I can offer you one more chart before you go.

When you create and follow a budget, you apply organizing skills where there once were none. Budgeting is a form of project management, which is a form of organizing, meaning it's just another process improvement to be made and has no reflection on your character or your worth as a person.

If you've completed all of the projects in this book, you now have all the data you need to build a budget. When you do and you start to use it, you will have transitioned from a passive use of money to a more intentional, informed, and active application of your financial resources. You'll be spending your money in an organized manner.

Beginning at the Beginning

Go back, way back, to Figure 1.4 in Chapter 1: the income and expense tracking document. Take another look at the anticipated versus actual columns of that spreadsheet. How accurate have your projections been?

Now look again at the calculations you've made in this chapter. How did your profit-and-loss statement in Figure 8.1 turn out? How many expenses did you find yourself stuck with in Figure 8.2? How daunting are the loans in your liabilities chart from Figure 8.3? What debt-to-income ratio did you come up with in Figure 8.4? This can be scary stuff, and by now I bet you know what I'm going to say: Self-loathing will get you nowhere. Talking it out with a therapist could be very helpful, and making plans with a financial advisor will help you solve complicated financial problems. So, take a deep breath and plan to enlist help as needed.

Many of my clients thought they would never get organized. They thought the little bit we accomplished each week would never be enough. But they kept chipping away, and gradually they began to see a difference. You can, too. You might have a lot of work to do to get your finances into the shape you want, but if you create a budget and start using it today, by this time next year you'll be amazed at how far you've come. Think a year is too long to wait? Look at it this way: That year is going to pass one way or another; why not be better off financially by then?

Designing Your Budget

Considering everything you've now learned about your finances, spend some time thinking about priorities. What's the single most important goal to accomplish now? What's second, and what's third? Determine your top three financial priorities, and use them to inform your new budget.

You can build on one of the tools you already created, use a function built in to your money-management software, or start from scratch using a chart like the one in Figure 8.5. However you choose to build your budget, be sure it includes these components:

- A place to record both anticipated and actual net income.
- A place to record both the anticipated amount and the actual amount of every expenditure.
- Budgeted amounts that are based on the most accurate information available to you.
- Plenty of reality: Do budget for an occasional movie or dinner out; don't think you'll be able to deny yourself all of life's pleasures for an extended period of time. At the same time, budget for unexpected expenses, too; don't count on making it through the next year without at least one minor disaster.

Figure 8.5 shows an example of a budget template, but don't use this one! It's crucial that you make your own budget template, customized precisely to your needs, where you can list all of your expenses, in your own words, rather than trying to fit yourself into someone else's lines and language.

Now comes the creative portion of our budgeting exercise: plugging in the numbers. Organizationally, this is no different from arranging boxes on a shelf. You have a finite amount of space (money) and some items (expenses) that need to go into it. If everything won't fit, you must either increase your space (income) or decrease your stuff (expenses).

Suppose you discover that it's not all going to fit, and you have no way of increasing your space. There's only one answer: Some stuff will have to go. But how do you decide what to eliminate?

Start with the three priorities you identified a few paragraphs back. Maybe one of them was saving for a much-needed new roof, or contributing to your retirement fund, or getting out from under credit card debt by paying more than the minimum each month. What expenses are related to those priorities? Plug those in first.

FIGURE 8.5

Here is an example of a budget template containing the necessary components of budgeted amounts, actual amounts, and itemized expenses. It is very important that you make your own customized template based on your unique needs.

My Budget for _____ 20__ through _____ 20__						
My top financial priority:						
My second financial priority:						
My third financial priority:						
	Month 1:		Month 2:		Month 3:	
INCOME	Budget	Actual	Budget	Actual	Budget	Actual
Joe						
Sue						
TOTAL INCOME						
EXPENSES	Budget	Actual	Budget	Actual	Budget	Actual
Loans & Credit Cards						
Mortgage 1						
Mortgage 2						
Car Payment						
Sue's Visa						
Joe's MasterCard						
Taxes & Utilities						
Property Tax						
Electric						
Gas						
Water						
Cable						
Phone/Internet						
Cellphone						
Insurance						
Auto Insurance						
Homeowner's Insurance						
Life Insurance						
Household & Pet Svcs						
Lawn/Snow Service						
Vet						
Personal						
Gym membership						
~SAVE FOR~						
New Roof ($5000)						
~PURCHASES~						
Groceries/Household Items						
Other: _____						
Other: _____						
Other: _____						
Other: _____						
TOTAL EXPENSES						

Of the remaining items, pull out the ones that you must pay to avoid the direst of consequences. Add these into your budget. Where do you stand now? Is there still some room? Continue adding items, most important first.

Getting pretty full? Okay, maybe you can do some rearranging. Of the items you already put in, can you make any of them smaller? Could you shave a couple dollars off the phone bill, or even drop your home line and use just your cell phone? Look for some creative solutions to fit as much as you realistically can into your budget.

After you've wedged in all that's going to fit, commit to that budget. Start living it. You've spent hours and hours to get this far, so don't undo all of your progress by straying from the wisdom you've gained and then applied in developing your budget.

SAVING THE OLD-FASHIONED WAY

This might be hard to fathom in our electronic world, but when it comes to saving money, some people still do best with a simple envelopes-and-cash system.

Some people are what organizers call *kinesthetic* or *tactile*, meaning they relate to objects best by touching them. If you prefer cash over cards and you have a hard time thinking of it as real money unless it's in the form of greenbacks in your hand, you're probably kinesthetic/tactile.

Now, obviously, there are significant drawbacks to keeping all of your money in cash form. However, if you really are drawn to the idea, you can apply it in limited ways that might be effective for you. For example, if you're having a tough time saving, you could withdraw a predetermined amount of cash each payday and divide it among several envelopes, such as Home Repairs, Vacation, and New Car.

Don't be afraid to try unconventional systems: If it works for you, it's fine.

Trimming Expenses Gets Easier

As you're ranking your expenses in order of importance, you might find that it's now easier to eliminate some items you used to consider more important. This is a common phenomenon in organizing that occurs when you bring all items of one category or group together.

For example, suppose your clothes aren't at all organized. You have garments all over your house, and you're not sure what you have or need. You walk around picking up items of clothing, one at a time, and with each one you decide you should keep it. Enter the organizer: I gather up all of your clothes, sort them into categories, and bring you one category at a time to weed out. You had no idea that you owned six black sweaters, but now that you see them all together, it's easy to choose the two best and toss the other four.

The lesson: You can't make an informed decision regarding what to keep and what to eliminate until you can see everything you have all at once in each category. It's true with clothes, dishes, CDs, and knick-knacks; it's true with all forms of paper, from magazines to tax records; and it's definitely true with expenditures!

FOCUSING ON THE BIG PICTURE

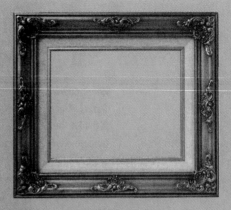

To make your budget work, as with any organizing system, you need to retain the vision of the Big Picture. If you're hit with a craving for a $5 premium coffee, you might think five bucks is no big deal and indulge. But if you've retained the Big Picture, you'll remember the more important thing that you budgeted for instead of that coffee, and you'll pass it up without feeling deprived.

Keep that Big Picture fresh in your mind by reviewing your budget almost constantly—every day is not unreasonable. If your dream were to be a singer, wouldn't you sing every day? You're trying to develop a new skill and change a whole group of habits, so it makes sense that you would need daily practice and reinforcement to succeed.

And that's as far as my organizing abilities can take you on this road. If you're ready for more advanced advice or assistance, it's time to talk to a financial expert. You can find plenty of free or low-cost information on the Internet (always remembering to take everything with a grain of salt); the Motley Fool site (www.fool.com) is especially comprehensive and comprehensible. Suze Orman's many books and tapes are very popular for guidance on budgeting and wealth-building and, of course, there's my favorite, *The Millionaire Next Door* (see the following sidebar). For one-on-one assistance, search the phone book or Internet for experts in the field of financial management, budgeting, or debt counseling. Continue to educate yourself with books, Web sites, conversations with friends, and consultations with experts. This is one venue where knowledge is most definitely power.

FURTHER READING: *THE MILLIONAIRE NEXT DOOR*

Here's a book that changed my thinking: *The Millionaire Next Door: The Surprising Secrets of America's Wealthy*, by Thomas J. Stanley (no relation to me) and William D. Danko. Their concept of PAWs (prodigious accumulators of wealth) versus UAWs (under-accumulators of wealth) opened my eyes to what wealth really is and how people acquire it. The descriptions of America's average millionaires (hint: most of them wear denim and drive unremarkable cars) were a revelation to me and made me realize that wealth is attainable with the right mindset—no matter whether you were born rich or brilliant. If you're interested in learning how regular folks quietly, legally, and ethically amass large fortunes, read this book.

Summary

You're done! How do you feel? Optimistic? Excited? Exhausted? I'd expect all three—you've accomplished so much in this chapter and the entire book. Now you have not only great financial organizing tools and systems, but also newfound knowledge from analyzing your financial information in its now-organized configurations. You're ready to move from building to maintenance—from running with the merry-go-round to standing still and giving it the occasional push.

As you move into the maintenance phase, you'll continue to add knowledge, make improvements, and try new ideas. From here on out, if you commit to following your system and give yourself the information you need to make sound choices, you'll continue to make great progress. Look at you now: You've finished this book, just a couple hundred pages, and you're already miles ahead of where you started!

Conclusion

Now that you've completed this book, you're in a delicate position. You've introduced a multitude of organizational changes and improvements into your life, and it was invigorating—perhaps scary at times, but definitely productive. When you close the cover on this book, you enter the maintenance phase of your financial organizing efforts, and that phase brings its own challenges.

Some people enjoy the initial steps of organizing because they are exciting, and they dislike the maintenance phase because it's just the opposite. The setup is a whirlwind of ideas, revelations, and activities; when that's done, you're left with the methodical, relatively easy, relatively dull task of using your new systems.

Beware: Boredom can sabotage the best-laid organizing plans.

The "Just Do It" Factor

There is only so much that can be done to combat boredom. As I tell my clients, I can address 95% of any organizing problem, including assessing the existing situation, modifying the portions of it that are already working, adding new techniques and products for further improvement, delegating tasks to others when needed, and providing insight into the many psychological factors that impact whether you use your system. We've covered all of that ground in this book, meaning you're 95% of the way there in your goal of having organized finances for life.

The remaining 5% simply requires that you, as the Nike ads used to tell us, "just do it." This is the part that no one, not even a professional organizer, can do for you. Imagine it like a concert in which you're the star. Almost everything—95%—of what has to happen to make this concert a reality is addressed by a methodology that is already in place: The scheduling, promotion, ticket sales, sound and lighting, backup musicians, and travel arrangements all come together because of careful planning. But there's still that 5% that only you can provide: You have to show up and sing.

Use Your System

Remember the icons you saw throughout the book reminding you of some universal organizing principles? "Show up and sing" is another way of saying, "Use your system." Now that you have a great system, use it! If you don't—if you stay away too long—your system will suffer from neglect because you will forget exactly how to use it. Your bills will fall behind, you'll start getting overdrafts again, and your filing will pile up, all because the world's greatest system still needs you to provide that crucial 5%.

So, "use your system" is the key principle to keep in mind as you move forward. Over time, as you sustain your newfound organization, you will occasionally need to upgrade or modify it, and for that, you'll benefit from remembering the other organizing principles: "be consistent," "have a home," and "organized enough." These are equally important in all forms of organizing, not just finances, so carry them with you as you tackle new projects and you'll find that they give you a head start on organizing absolutely anything.

Here are some ways these principles will help you for the rest of your financial life. Keep them in mind for other organizing projects as well.

Have a Home

Consider all of the materials that you used as you worked through the chapters of this book. Does every item have a home set aside for it? Anything that needs to be put away should have a designated place where it belongs—a home. Materials related to your finances that need a home include all of your records, supplies for bill-paying, incoming bills, and disks containing your backup files. A home can be a physical space, for example a file drawer, horizontal stacker, fire safe, desk drawer, or your wallet or purse. For data that exists only electronically, a space on your hard drive or on disk will be its home. Now look around your mind. How much stuff up there is homeless? How many cash transactions, account numbers, and budget amounts are floating around in your head like bobbing apples? These need homes, too. Get them out of the apple tub, dry them off, and put them into your financial software, income and expense tracking document, computer files, or wherever else they belong. As the water in the apple tub settles, so will your thoughts go from choppy waves ("Yikes, I'm forgetting something!") to a placid lake ("Ah, peace: It's all recorded").

Be Consistent

In this book I've given you some examples of how straying from a system often results in forgotten or lost items. You've surely seen this concept in your own life: We don't realize what creatures of habit we are until someone disrupts one of those habits. Even something as simple as holidays that throw off the mail delivery or trash pickup can start a chain reaction and make us feel off-kilter the entire day.

It can be humbling to accept this reality, but it's important to do so: Once your system is working, you need to relinquish control to it and trust that you had good reasons for setting it up as you did, even if you can't remember those reasons at the moment. When I try to hold a transaction in memory until it's convenient to write it down, invariably I forget it until it pops up on my bank statement. This is why I have a system that requires me to record every transaction, and it works perfectly as long as I adhere to it.

If a component of your financial organizing system alerts you to do something, do it: Trust that you were right when you built that system, and follow it, even when (*especially* when) you're distracted and don't want to take the time. If you determine that your system really does need a change, make that change, but do so carefully, which much forethought, not on the fly as you're running your day.

Be Organized Enough

And finally, my favorite, the organizing principle that will set you free: Be only as organized as you need to be. No matter what event you're planning, what data you're capturing, or what items you're arranging, always remember that organizing for the sake of organizing is wasteful. Resist the temptation to show everyone you're "more organized than thou." Do what works for you and don't worry about whether it's good enough for someone else.

With any organizing upgrade you make, ask yourself what it will gain you. If you consider adding a layer of complexity to your budgeting system, for example by switching from monthly to weekly, make sure the advantages of that change are worth the disruption of your already-functioning system. Perhaps more detail will turn out to be just what you need, but for someone else it would be over the top. But perhaps what you have is just enough, and you're simply craving some sort of change.

As long as you can find any financial document or bit of data within a minute or two, know how much money you have and where it's going, and remember to pay the bills on time, congratulations! You're organized enough.

Farewell

We've reached the end, so it's time for me to wish you well and congratulate you on all you've accomplished. I hope what you've learned in this book will benefit you for a very long time and will encourage you to add more organization where it's needed in other areas of your life. Best wishes for your newly organized financial future!

Further Resources

Consult the resources listed here for further advice and information on money management and financial issues including budgeting, use of credit, obtaining a loan, reducing debt, investing, and much more. Also listed are all products and services referenced in this book, plus resources for finding a professional organizer to help you work toward your organizing goals.

Products and Services Recommended in This Book

Books

- Stanley, Thomas J., and William D. Danko. *The Millionaire Next Door*. Pocket Books, 1998.

- Fellman, Wilma. *Finding a Career That Works for You*. Independent Publishers Group, 2000.

- Ramundo, Kelly, Kate, and Peggy. *You Mean I'm Not Lazy, Stupid or Crazy?! A Self-Help Book for Adults with Attention Deficit Disorder*. Simon & Schuster, 1993.

Data Management Products and Services

- **iBackup**—Online storage site for backing up your computer files (www.ibackup.com)

- **Microsoft Excel**—Spreadsheet program with large data capacity and powerful calculation functions (www.microsoft.com/Office/Excel/prodinfo/default.mspx)

- **Microsoft Word**—Word-processing software that allows you to make lists and create tables as part of your financial organization (www.microsoft.com/office/word/prodinfo/default.mspx)

Junk Mail Management Services

- **Direct Marketing Association Mail Preference Service**—Write to the Direct Marketing Association's Mail Preference Service to be added to its name-removal file. Use the online form or send a letter with your full name, complete home address, telephone number, and signature. (www.dmaconsumers.org/cgi/offmailinglist#regform) or Box 643, Carmel, NY 10512)

- **National Opt-Out Center**—Contact the National Opt-Out Center to stop unwanted credit card offers. (888-567-8688)

- **U.S. Postal Service**—Use Form 1500 to prevent sexually oriented advertising from being mailed to you. The form is available from your local post office or online at www.usps.com/forms/pdf/ps1500.pdf. (www.usps.gov)

Money Management Products

- **Money by Microsoft and Quicken by Intuit**—The Quicken and Money families of products offer options for users at various levels of expertise, from basic checking account management to small business needs. (www.microsoft.com/money/default.asp and www.intuit.com)

Organizing Products

- **File folders**—The most common filing method uses hanging folders in file drawers, but other options can work equally well. Use end-tab folders such as those made by Smead (available at www.staples.com) to create an in-sight, vertical filing system on a shelf or countertop.

- **File racks**—Vertical incline file racks allow you to see your folders while keeping them neat and upright. Several models are available at www.staples.com.

- **Fire safes**—A fire safe is the best in-home option for protecting your irreplaceable documents and backup disks. The Sentry FIRE-SAFE Data Storage Security Chest Model 1710 or Data Storage Security File Model 6720 promises protection for paper and computer media. See www.sentrysafe.com.

- **Personal digital assistants (PDAs)**—The Palm Pilot (www.palm.com) was the first PDA, and now dozens of PDAs are available. The basic functions of each are the calendar, address book, to-do list, and notepad, but many also offer Internet connectivity, email access, and digital recording options.

- **Shredders**—A shredder is essential for keeping your private information out of the hands of identity thieves. Choose a cross-cut shredder with a sheet capacity and running time that are adequate for your needs. One to consider is the Fellowes PS60C-2 (www.fellowes.com), which shreds eight sheets at a time into 5/32" × 1 3/8" particles and can handle credit cards, staples, and paper clips.

Financial Information and Counseling

AARP

Contact: www.aarp.org/financial

This site, which is open to nonmembers, offers an abundance of finance-related information, including calculators for strategizing your retirement savings plan.

American Savings Education Council

Contact: www.asec.org

This nonprofit organization's Web site includes a section of handy savings tools and enlightening financial planning calculators.

Credit Bureaus

Contact: Equifax (800-685-1111 or www.equifax.com), Experian (888-397-3742 or www.experian.com), and TransUnion (800-888-4213 or www.tuc.com)

Obtain copies of your credit reports from each of the three credit reporting agencies to check for errors and identity theft.

Debtors Anonymous

Contact: www.debtorsanonymous.org

This organization employs the 12-step approach popularized by Alcoholics Anonymous to help people learn to control their spending. The Web site features a quiz to determine whether you are a compulsive debtor and has some resources for suggested reading.

Fannie Mae Foundation

Contact: www.fanniemae.com **or 800-732-6643**

As stated on its Web site, Fannie Mae's "public mission, and our defining goal, is to help more families achieve the American Dream of homeownership. We do that by providing financial products and services that make it possible for low-, moderate-, and middle-income families to buy homes of their own." The Web site includes calculation tools for determining the complete cost of a house and how much you can afford to spend, a glossary of real estate and mortgage terminology, links to Fannie Mae-approved lenders, and many more resources for first-time home buyers.

Identity Theft Resource Center

Contact: www.idtheftcenter.org **or 858-693-7935**

A nonprofit resource for information on preventing and recovering from identity theft.

InCharge Debt Solutions (formerly Profina Debt Solutions)

Contact: debtsolutions.incharge.org **or 800-565-8953**

InCharge describes itself as "a non-profit, community-service organization offering confidential and professional credit counseling, debt management, and financial education programs to individuals nationwide." There are a number of similarly described organizations in existence (search the Internet for "financial counseling"); some offer free services and others charge a fee or extract a percentage of any debt consolidation they perform for you.

Internal Revenue Service

Contact: www.irs.gov

The IRS is the best source for answers to tax-related questions. Its Web site allows electronic access to all IRS publications and forms and includes instructions for obtaining copies of past tax returns and guidance on how long to retain tax-related financial records.

Investor's Clearinghouse

Contact: www.investoreducation.org

Sponsored by the nonprofit Alliance for Investor Education, the Investor's Clearinghouse Web site features a library of articles in categories including Investing Basics, Young Investors, Older Investors, Scams, and Getting Help.

Managing My Money.com

Contact: www.managingmymoney.com

This Web site, funded by the Community Action Partnership and the National Endowment for Financial Education (NEFE), offers free advice and articles on topics including goal-setting, living within your means, finding ways to save on essentials like food and clothing, tips for homeowners and renters, and conducting a successful job search. The site also features a comprehensive list of further resources.

The Motley Fool

Contact: www.fool.com

The Motley Fool began as a newsletter dedicated to readers helping each other to make better financial decisions and has since grown to include a Web site, numerous books, and *The Motley Fool Radio Show* hosted by Motley Fool founders David and Tom Gardner and broadcast regularly on National Public Radio. This group is distinguished by an irreverent, unintimidating approach to managing finances.

MSN Money

Contact: moneycentral.msn.com

This Web site is formatted like a newspaper, with finance-related news and feature articles that change daily. The site also includes special reports and in-depth sections on investing, banking, planning, and taxes.

Suze Orman

Contact: www.suzeorman.com

Orman is a popular financial advisor, with books on a wide variety of money-management topics, an informative Web site, and a television program, *The Suze Orman Show*, on CNBC.

Quicken

Contact: www.quicken.com

This site features specifications on Quicken financial software plus general money-management information.

Stopping Overshopping

Contact: www.stoppingovershopping.com

This site offers advice, support, and resources on compulsive shopping.

U.S. Courts

Contact: www.uscourts.gov/bankruptcycourts.html

This government site provides information on how to file for bankruptcy.

Professional Organizing Information and Referrals

National Association of Professional Organizers (NAPO)

Contact: www.napo.net **or 847-375-4746**

NAPO is The Organizing Authority with more than 2,200 members throughout the United States, Canada, and seven other countries. The NAPO Web site features a free, automated referral system that allows users to search for an organizer by specialty, geographic region, and many other criteria.

National Study Group on Chronic Disorganization (NSGCD)

Contact: www.nsgcd.org

The NSGCD provides referrals to professional organizers who specialize in helping chronically disorganized clients and those with additional needs due to physical or mental disabilities.

Professional Organizers in Canada (POC)

Contact: www.organizersincanada.com

Incorporated in 2001, POC is evidence of the growing popularity of professional organizing as both a service and a career. POC offers a free Web-based referral service and currently has more than 200 members throughout Canada.

Sample Finance Forms

Income & Expense Tracking Spreadsheet (see also Chapter 1, Figure 1.4)

	JAN				FEB			
INCOME	Expected Date	Expected Amt	Actual Date	Actual Amt	Expected Date	Expected Amt	Actual Date	Actual Amt
___'s Income, week 1								
___'s Income, week 2								
___'s Income, week 3								
___'s Income, week 4								
___'s Income, week 1								
___'s Income, week 2								
___'s Income, week 3								
___'s Income, week 4								
TOTAL INCOME								
EXPENSES	Expected Date	Expected Amt	Actual Date	Actual Amt	Expected Date	Expected Amt	Actual Date	Actual Amt
Loans & Credit Cards								
Mortgage								
Car Payment								
___ Credit Card								
___ Credit Card								
Taxes & Utilities								
Property Tax								
Electric								
Gas								
Water								
Cable								
Phone/Internet								
Cellphone								
Insurance								
Auto								
Homeowner's								
Life								
Household & Pet Svcs								
Lawn/Snow Service								
Vet								
Personal								
Gym membership								
~SAVE FOR~								
New Roof ($5000)								
~PURCHASES~								
Groceries/Household Items								
TOTAL EXPENSES								

Medical Bill Tracking Spreadsheet (see also Chapter 3, Figure 3.2)

My insurance notes: $_____ copay, $_____ deductible

Event Date	Description	Pd at Site								
			Bill 1: Biller:_____	Date Due	Total	Minus Insurance Pd	Amt I Owe	Amt Pd	Date Pd	Notes:
			Date Rec'd							
			Bill 2: Biller:_____	Date Due	Total	Minus Insurance Pd	Amt I Owe	Amt Pd	Date Pd	Notes:
			Date Rec'd							
			Bill 3: Biller:_____	Date Due	Total	Minus Insurance Pd	Amt I Owe	Amt Pd	Date Pd	Notes:
			Date Rec'd							
			Bill 4: Biller:_____	Date Due	Total	Minus Insurance Pd	Amt I Owe	Amt Pd	Date Pd	Notes:
			Date Rec'd							
			Bill 5: Biller:_____	Date Due	Total	Minus Insurance Pd	Amt I Owe	Amt Pd	Date Pd	Notes:
			Date Rec'd							
			Bill 6: Biller:_____	Date Due	Total	Minus Insurance Pd	Amt I Owe	Amt Pd	Date Pd	Notes:
			Date Rec'd							

Event Date	Description	Pd at Site								
			Bill 1: Biller:_____	Date Due	Total	Minus Insurance Pd	Amt I Owe	Amt Pd	Date Pd	Notes:
			Date Rec'd							
			Bill 2: Biller:_____	Date Due	Total	Minus Insurance Pd	Amt I Owe	Amt Pd	Date Pd	Notes:
			Date Rec'd							
			Bill 3: Biller:_____	Date Due	Total	Minus Insurance Pd	Amt I Owe	Amt Pd	Date Pd	Notes:
			Date Rec'd							
			Bill 4: Biller:_____	Date Due	Total	Minus Insurance Pd	Amt I Owe	Amt Pd	Date Pd	Notes:
			Date Rec'd							
			Bill 5: Biller:_____	Date Due	Total	Minus Insurance Pd	Amt I Owe	Amt Pd	Date Pd	Notes:
			Date Rec'd							
			Bill 6: Biller:_____	Date Due	Total	Minus Insurance Pd	Amt I Owe	Amt Pd	Date Pd	Notes:
			Date Rec'd							

Belongings Inventory (see also Chapter 6, Figure 6.2)

Item	Source	Acq. Date	Orig. Price/ Value	Replacemt Value (What ins. should pay)	Resale Value (eBay?)	Notes:

Web Shopping Sites Spreadsheet (see also Chapter 7, Figure 7.2)										
Company	Web site	Category:	Category:	Category:	Category:	Category:	Category:	Category:	Category:

Budget Template (see also Chapter 8, Figure 8.6)

My Budget for _____ 20__ through _____ 20__

My top financial priority:

My second financial priority:

My third financial priority:

	Month 1: _____		Month 2: _____		Month 3: _____	
INCOME	Budget	Actual	Budget	Actual	Budget	Actual
From _____						
From _____						
TOTAL INCOME						
EXPENSES	Budget	Actual	Budget	Actual	Budget	Actual
Loans & Credit Cards						
Taxes & Utilities						
Insurance						
Household & Pet Svcs						
Personal						
~SAVE FOR~						
~PURCHASES~						
TOTAL EXPENSES						

Index

A

AARP (American Association Retired Persons) Web site, 145

net worth calculator, 130

airline miles, tracking as non-cash asset, 40

all-paper bill payment system

medical bills processing, 55-56

process steps, 54-55

alphabetizing frequent files versus categorizing, 86

American Savings Education Council Web site, 145

archive files

creating, 92

destroy dates, 93-94

document separation, 93

IRS records, 93

organizing, 83

storage containers, 95

ATM cash advances, receipt collection, 16-17

attention deficit disorder (ADD), effect on impulse buying, 120

automatic bill payments versus electronic bill payments, 59

B

backing up financial data, 41

CD size capacities, 43

disk size capacities, 43

disk storage location, 43-45

method selection, 41-42

rewritable CD size capacities, 43

balancing checking accounts

by hand, 30-33

computer options, 35

investigation of discrepancies, 33-34

overview, 29-30

software options, 35-37

bankruptcy, declaration information, 129

banks

checking accounts, balancing methods, 29-37

overdrafts, avoiding via safety valve accounts, 50-52

statements, requesting, 34

bills and on-time payments

all-paper system, 54-56

electronic versus automatic, 59

evaluating your approach, 50

jogger approach, 49

methods, 52

online-based system, 58-59

reasons for delays, 49

required supplies, 54

software-based system, 57-58

sprinter approach, 49

storage location, 73

strategies, 48-49

system comfort, 59-60

up-to-date financial data, 53

use of professional services, 60

use of safety valve accounts, 50-52

books

Finding a Career That Works for You, 144

The Millionaire Next Door – The Surprising Secrets of America's Wealthy, 138

bounced checks. *See* over-drafts

budgets

book resources, 137

components of, 134-135

customization of, 134-135

expense analysis, 136-137

organization of, 133-137

Web site resources, 137

business-related financial software, 37

by-month filing system, 89

C

calculating

debt-to-income ratios, 131-132

net worth, 130

personal profits/losses, 126-128

total debt, 128-129

cash tracking

ATM cash advances, 16-17

expense tracking document creation, 20-24

income tracking document creation, 19-23

invisibility of, 10

joint account management strategies, 26-28

management issues, 10

organizational system selection, 11-12

overview, 9-11

paying by check, 18-19

paying by credit card, 18

receipt collection methods, 12-15

receipt destination spots, 16

recording of daily transaction, 17-18

spreadsheet components, 20-22

time issues, 11

catalogs, clutter reduction, 114-116

categories (filing)

Room by Room, 101-102

Frequent Files, 86-89

CDs (compact discs)

financial data, backing up, 41-42

size capacities, 43

checking accounts, balancing

by hand, 30-33

computer options, 35

investigation of discrepancies, 33-34

software options, 35-37

statements, requesting, 34

checking credit reports, 61

collecting receipts

ATM cash advances, 16-17

destination spots, 16

importance of, 13-15

colleges, financial aid (Upromise.org Web site), 40

computers as paperless storage system, 81-82

controlling daily mail, 66-67

    elimination of junk mail, 67-69

credit cards

    receipts, collecting, 18

    solicitations in junk mail, 70

credit reporting agencies

    Equifax, 61

    Experian, 61

    TransUnion, 61

    Web site resources, 145

D

daily mail

    bills, storage location, 73

    categories, 68-69

    control strategies, 66-69

    handling with File/Act/Toss model, 74

    junk mail inserts, handling, 71

    magazines, storage locations, 73-74

daily transactions (receipts), recording, 17-18

debt-to-income ratios

    calculating, 131-132

    house payment affordability, 132

    safe percentages, 132

Debtors Anonymous Web site, 129, 146

debts

    assessments, 128-129

    bankruptcy, declaring, 129

    Debtors Anonymous Web site, 129

    elements of, 131

    Identity Theft Resource Center Web site, 146

    InCharge Debt Solutions Web site, 146

destroy dates (archive files), 93-94

Direct Marketing Association (DMA) Web site, 144

    adding to junk mail name-removal file, 69

discrepancies in bank account balances, 33-34

disks

    financial data, backing up, 41-42

    size capacities, 43

documents, filing, 82

    archive files, 83, 92-95

    by-month system, 89

    frequent files, 82-92

    household files, 82

    project and research files, 83

    room-by-room files, 83, 97-107

    safe storage files, 83, 95

    storage options, 78-82

DVDs (digital video discs), collections, list maintenance, 117

E

electronic bill payments versus automatic bill payments, 59

envelopes-and-cash system, money saving method, 136

Equifax Web site, 61

expenditures, viewing against income statements, 126-128

expense tracking documents

    category set up, 23-24

    creating, 19-20

    expected dates/expenses, 24-25

Experian Web site, 61

F

Fannie Mae Web site, 146

Fellowes.com Web site, 71, 145

file folders, vertical storage systems, 80-81

File/Act/Toss model, daily mail handling strategies, 74

filing groups, 82

    archive files, 83, 92-95

    by-month system, 89

    frequent files, 82-92

    household files, 82

    project and research files, 83

    room-by-room files, 83, 97-107

    safe storage files, 83-95

How can we make this index more useful? Email us at indexes@quepublishing.com

filing/piling system, 80-81

financial advisors, use of, 26

financial counseling

advisors, use of, 26

Web site resources, 145-148

financial data, backing up, 41-45

financial software

checking accounts, 35-36

common features, 36-37

data, backing up, 41-42

selection criteria, 35-40

Web sites, 37

fire safes

financial data storage, 44

Sentry Safes Web site, 44, 145

folders

frequent files

filing process, 91-92

hanging style, 90-91

labeling, 90

room-by-room files, creating, 101

frequent files

categorizing versus alphabetizing, 86

filing process, 91-92

folder labels, 90

hanging folders, 90-91

naming, 87

organizing, 82-84

subcategories, 87-89

G

gift-giving lists, maintaining, 117-120

grocery lists

benefits of, 111-112

mapping out, 112-114

grouping documents, 82

archive files, 83, 92-95

by-month system, 89

frequent files, 82-92

household files, 82

project and research files, 83

room-by-room files, 83, 97-107

safe storage files, 83, 95

H

handling daily mail (File/Act/Toss model), 74

hanging folders (frequent files), 90-91

header rows in spreadsheets, 22

holiday shopping lists, maintaining, 117-120

house needs lists, maintaining, 121-122

house payments, 28/36 qualifying ratio (affordability), 132

household files, organizing, 82

household goods, expense analysis, 136-137

I

iBackup Web site, 144

online storage of financial data, 44-45

Identity Theft Resource Center Web site, 146

impulse buying

curbing, 116

effect of attention deficit disorder (ADD), 120

Stopping Over Shopping Web site, 116

InCharge Debt Solutions Web site, 146

income statements

elements of, 131

viewing against expenditures, 126-128

income tracking documents

creating, 19-20

setting up, 22-23

incoming paper management. *See also* **bills; junk mail**

daily mail, control strategies, 66-69

importance of daily control, 65-66

junk mail, handling, 69-71

paper life cycle, 65

sources other than mail, handling, 75

instruction manuals, organizing, 98-99

insurance, personal property inventories, 104

requirements of, 106-107

Internet banking. *See* **online bill payments**

Intuit Web site, 37, 144

investment/financial software, 37

Investor's Clearinghouse Web site, 147

IRS (Internet Revenue Service)

records, destroy dates, 94

tax returns, copies, requesting, 34

Web site, 34

J - K

joint checking accounts

financial advisors, use of, 26

management strategies, 26-28

money-handling strategies, 50-52

junk mail

acceptable forms of, 68-69

eliminating, 67-69

inserts within real mail, handling, 71

lists, removal from, 69

sexually oriented advertising (SOA), stopping, 70

shredding guidelines, 71-73

unwanted credit card solicitations, 70

Web site reduction resources, 144

L

labeling frequent files, 90

lists

DVD collections, 117

gift-giving, 117-120

grocery, 111-114

holiday shopping, 117-120

house needs, 121-122

shopping, 111-114

loans, debt calculations, 128-129

M

magazines, storage locations, 73-74

Managing My Money.com Web site, 147

mapping

grocery stores for list creation, 112-114

shopping stores for list creation, 112-114

medical bills, management and organization of, 55-56

Microsoft Excel, 144

Microsoft Money Web site, 37, 144

Microsoft Word, 144

The Millionaire Next Door – The Surprising Secrets of America's Wealthy, 138

money, tracking

ATM cash advances, 16-17

expense tracking documents, 19-25

income tracking documents, 19-23

invisibility of, 10

joint accounts, management strategies, 26-28

management issues, 10

organizational system selection, 11-12

overview, 9-11

paying by check, 18-19

paying by credit card, 18

receipt collection methods, 12-16

recording of daily transactions, 17-18

spreadsheet components, 20-22

time issues, 11

Web site resources, 144

Motley Fool Web site, 137, 147

MSN Money Web site, 147

N - O

National Opt-Out Center Web site, 144

net worth, calculating, 130

non-cash assets, 40

non-mail papers, handling, 75

offsite storage (financial data), 43-44

fire safes, 44

safe deposit box, 44

work locales, 44

on-time bill payments

evaluating your approach, 50

jogger approach, 49

methods, 52-60

reasons for delays, 49

required supplies, 54

sprinter approach, 49

strategies, 48-49

up-to-date financial data, 53

use of professional services, 60

use of safety valve accounts, 50-52

online bill payments

issues to consider, 52

process steps, 58-59

online shopping

impulse buying, curbing, 116

paper catalogs, clutter reduction, 114-116

transaction records, maintaining, 122

online storage (financial data), iBackup Web site, 44-45

open filing system, 80-81

organization system

receipt collection methods, 12-16

recording of daily transactions, 17-18

selection criteria, 11-12

organizational products, Web site resources

Fellowes.com, 145

Palm.com, 145

Sentry Safes, 145

Staples, 145

Orman, Suze, 137

overdrafts (bounced checks), avoiding, 50-52

P

page sizes of spreadsheets, setting, 22

Palm.com Web site, 145

paper catalogs, clutter reduction, 114-116

paper planners versus PDAs, 117

paper shredders, 145

paperless storage system, 81-82

papers, storage options, 78-79

filing/piling system, 80-81

open filing system, 80-81

paperless system, 81-82

pending items, 85

piling system, 79

PAWs (prodigious accumulators of wealth), 138

PDAs (personal digital assistants)

DVD collections, list maintenance, 117

holiday supply lists, maintaining, 118-119

Palm.com, 145

versus paper planners, 117

Peachtree Accounting Web site, 37

pending items, storing, 85

personal finances

budgets, 133-137

debt-to-income ratios, calculating, 131-132

debts, assessment of, 128-129

on-time bill payments, 52-60

personal profits/losses, calculating, 126-128

saving money, envelopes-and-cash system, 136

spending patterns, analysis of, 130

Web site resources, 137

personal gift lists, maintaining, 120

personal profits/losses, calculating, 126-128

personal property inventory (room-by-room files)

building, 97-99

categories, 101-102

creating, 104

document saving criteria, 102-103

filing process, 102

folder creation, 101

gathering, 100

insurance requirements, 106-107

maintenance of, 103, 107

space listings, 100-101

videotaping, 104-105

written entry via computer, 106

piling system (document storage), 79

professional bill payment services, 60

project files, organizing, 83

property inventories (room-by-room files), 104

insurance requirements, 106-107

maintenance of, 107

videotaping, 104-105

written entry via computer, 106

purchases (receipt collection)

paying by check, 18-19

paying by credit card, 18

Q - R

Quicken.com Web site, 147

receipts

ATM cash advances, 16-17

collection methods, 12-13

destination spots, 16

importance of collecting, 13-15

purchases by check, 18-19

purchases by credit card, 18

recording of daily transactions, 17-18

room-by-room files, organizing, 98-99

reconciliation. *See* **balancing checking accounts**

records for online shopping, 122

recurring transactions, 36

reports and budgeting features (financial software), 36

research files, organizing, 83

rewritable CDs

financial data, backing up, 41-42

size capacities, 43

room-by-room files

building, 98-99

categories, 101-102

document saving criteria, 102-103

filing process, 102

folder creation, 101

gathering, 100

maintenance of, 103

organizing, 83, 97-98

property inventories, 104-107

space listings, 100-101

S

safe deposit boxes, 44

safe storage files, organizing, 83, 95

safety valve accounts, overdraft avoidance, 50-52

saving files, documents to retain, 102-103

school-related papers, managing, 75

selecting financial software, criteria, 35-40

Sentry Safes Web site, 44, 145

shopping lists

benefits of, 111-112

mapping out, 112-114

shredders (paper), 71

shredding junk mail

Fellowes.com, 71

what to shred, 72-73

sign-and-return documents, managing, 75

software-based bill payment system, process steps, 57-58

spending patterns

    analysis of, 130

    StoppingOvershopping.com, 148

spreadsheets, income/expense tracking documents

    category creation, 22-24

    components of, 20-21

    creating, 19-20

    expected dates/expenses, 24-25

    header row creation, 22

    page selection, 22

    setting up, 23

    time increments, 21

Staples Web site, 145

StoppingOvershopping.com Web site, 148

storing

    bills, location of, 73

    documents, systems for, 78-82

    magazines, location of, 73-74

SuzeOrman.com Web site, 147

T

taxes

    copies of returns, requesting, 34

    IRS Web site resources, 146

time increments in spreadsheets, setting, 21

tracking money

    ATM cash advances, 16-17

    expense tracking documents, 20-24

    income tracking documents, 19-23

    invisibility of, 10

    management issues, 10

    organizational system selection, 11-12

    overview, 9-11

    paying by check, 18-19

    paying by credit card, 18

    receipt collection methods, 12-16

    recording of daily transactions, 17-18

    spreadsheet components, 20-22

    time issues, 11

transactions (daily)

    categories, tracking via financial software, 36

    online shopping, record maintenance, 122

TransUnion Web site, 61

28/36 qualifying ratio, house payment affordability, 132

U - V

U.S. Bankruptcy Court Web site, 129

U.S. Postal Service Web site, 144

    junk mail strategies, 70

UAWs (under-accumulators of wealth), 138

Upromise.org Web site, college financial aid, 40

vertical file systems, 80-81

videotaping personal property inventories, 104-105

W - Z

warranties, organizing, 98-99

wealth

    The Millionaire Next Door – The Surprising Secrets of America's Wealthy, 138

    PAWs (prodigious accumulators of wealth), 138

    UAWs (under-accumulators of wealth), 138

Web sites

AARP (American Association of Retired Persons), 130

credit reporting agencies, 145

Debtors Anonymous, 129

Direct Marketing Association, junk mail listing removal, 69

Equifax, 61

Experian, 61

financial counseling, 145-147

financial software, 37

IBackup, 44-45, 144

IRS, 34, 94, 146

junk mail reduction, 144

money management, 144

Motley Fool, 137

organizational products, 145

SentrySafe.com, 44

Stopping Over Shopping, 116

TransUnion, 61

U.S Bankruptcy Court, 129

U.S. Postal Service, 70

Upromise.org, 40

Do Even More
...In No Time

G et ready to cross off those items on your to-do list! *In No Time* helps you tackle the projects that you don't think you have time to finish. With shopping lists and step-by-step instructions, these books get you working toward accomplishing your goals.

Check out these other *In No Time* books, coming soon!

Start Your Own Home Business In No Time
ISBN: **0-7897-3224-6**
$16.95
September 2004

Plan a Fabulous Party In No Time
ISBN: **0-7897-3221-1**
$16.95
September 2004

Speak Basic Spanish In No Time
ISBN: **0-7897-3223-8**
$16.95
September 2004

Organize Your Garage In No Time
ISBN: **0-7897-3219-X**
$16.95
October 2004

Quick Family Meals In No Time
ISBN: **0-7897-3299-8**
$16.95
October 2004

Organize Your Family's Schedule In No Time
ISBN: **0-7897-3220-3**
$16.95
October 2004

Looking for professional organizing assistance?

Contact the Organizing Authority!

The National Association of Professional Organizers

Whether you need to organize your business or your home, NAPO members are ready to help you meet the challenge.

A professional organizer enhances the lives of clients by designing systems and processes using organizing principles and through transferring organizing skills. A professional organizer also educates the public on organizing solutions and the resulting benefits.

NAPO currently has more than 2,500 members throughout the U.S. and in 8 other countries ready to serve you.

For More Information or to Find a Professional Organizer in Your Area,

Visit the NAPO Web Site at **www.NAP.net**